Foreword by Dr. Pamela J. Pine

CALLED TO SERVE

STANDING WITH SURVIVORS AND PROTECTING CHILDREN STILL AT RISK

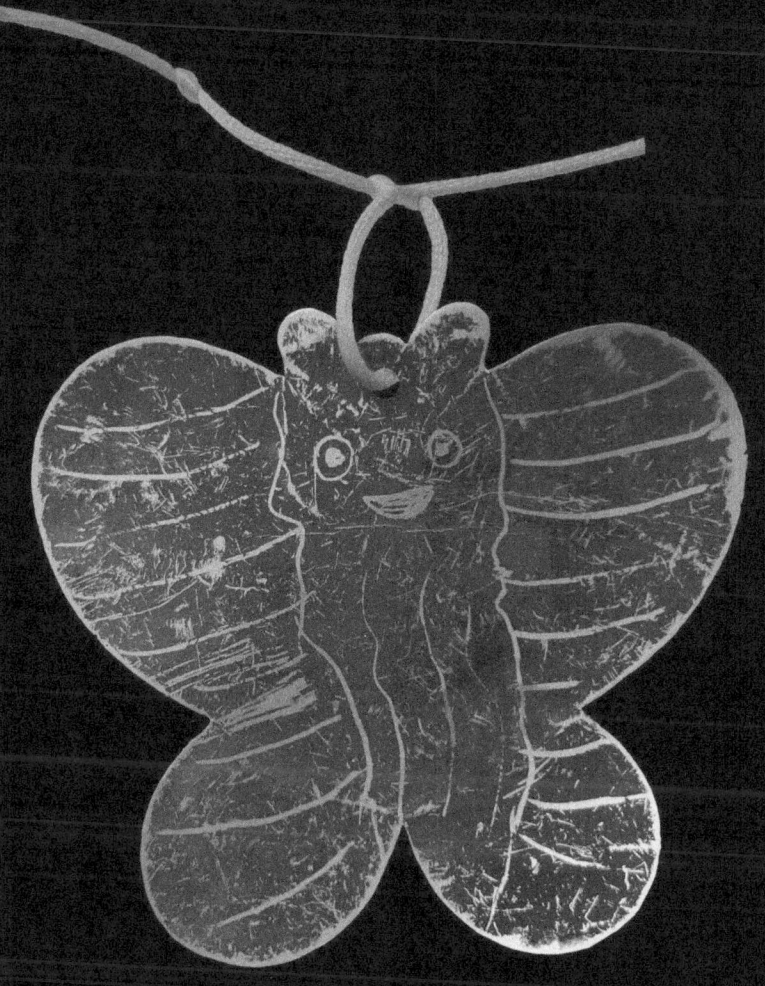

SUSAN L. ERNST

Called to Serve

Standing with Survivors and Protecting Children Still at Risk

©2025 Susan Ernst

Published by Brave Healer Productions

Cover and interior design by K.J. Kaschula

Paperback ISBN: 978-1-961493-36-0

E-book ISBN: 978-1-969999-00-0

Foreword by Dr. Pamela J. Pine

CALLED TO SERVE

STANDING WITH SURVIVORS AND PROTECTING CHILDREN STILL AT RISK

SUSAN L. ERNST

ABOUT THE BOOK COVER ART

The little butterfly on the cover may seem mysterious, but its meaning is revealed in Chapter 4. My thanks to K.J Kashula, whose vision brought to life a moment I will never forget—one that carries the heartbeat of my passion and devotion for the children I served.

CONTENT ADVISORY

This book contains references to child abuse, sex trafficking, and trauma. While these topics are approached with care and compassion, some sections may be emotionally difficult or triggering. If you or someone you know needs support, you'll find a list of trusted global resources at the end of this book.

A SPECIAL NOTE TO SURVIVORS:

If you are a survivor of abuse or exploitation, please know that this book was written with the most profound respect for your strength, your story, and your healing. You are not alone. While parts of this book may touch on painful realities, its purpose is to honor the resilience of children and the power of love, community, and hope.

Please feel free to engage with this book in whatever way supports your well-being. It's okay to pause, to skip sections, or to read with a trusted friend or counselor by your side. Your safety and healing come first.

If you are in crisis or need someone to talk to, help is available. Reach out to a licensed therapist, a local support organization, or a crisis hotline in your area.

This book is ultimately a tribute to healing, to the courage of those who serve, and to the survivors who continue to rise. You are seen. You are valued. You are loved.

You will see the following warning on some of the chapters that follow:

CONTENT WARNING:

This chapter contains depictions of child trafficking, including familial betrayal and exploitation. Reader discretion is advised.

DEDICATION

To the victims and survivors of child abuse and child sex trafficking—

This book is written with you in my heart.

Every word carries the weight of my grief, outrage, and my most profound compassion. Though I can never fully understand your pain, I see your courage, dignity, and your will to survive.

I'm not a healer, but I am a witness, and someone who cannot look away.

May this book find its way into the hands of those called to act, serve, protect, and restore. If it inspires even one heart to take a step, to do one brave thing to help end this atrocity, then it will have done what I prayed it would do.

With love, reverence, and hope for a world where every child is safe,

Susan Ernst

***

This book is dedicated to the memory of Don Brewster, Co-Founder of Agape International Missions, headquartered in Roseville, California.

Don Brewster approached every need as if it were his responsibility. In the fight against child sex trafficking, he didn't wait for others to step in—he acted, even when the odds were overwhelming. With remarkable clarity and conviction, he identified what was required and brought the right people together to meet the challenge. Those who had the privilege of serving alongside Don often found themselves rising beyond their perceived limits, encouraged by his steady confidence, unwavering support, and deep belief in the mission. I looked up to him with profound respect and gratitude.

Don was a radical listener and a kick-ass warrior. He is my hero!

To all those who give their time, resources, and hearts to serve the vulnerable in the far corners of the world. You show up not for praise or recognition, but because something deep within you says, "I can help." You step into unfamiliar places, face hard truths, and love through the ache of injustice. In rugged conditions and heartbreaking circumstances, you bring joy. Where there is pain, you offer presence. Where there's need, you offer yourself.

May your example continue to light the way for others.

***

To my extraordinary teammates—

Thank you for sharing this journey with me. Together we showed up, learned, and grew—each of us bringing our own gifts, skill sets, and hearts of service. What we created together was far more than a team; it was a circle of compassion, strength, and love.

***

To my beloved daughters, Laura and Alissa,

From the moment you entered my life, I felt an indescribable joy and a love that knows no bounds. I cherish our moments together—every shared laugh, every tear wiped away, all of it. With you, I've experienced the true meaning of unconditional love, and for that, I'm eternally thankful.

VI

My love for you transcends time and space; it's a constant, unwavering force that will forever bind us together.

Both of you have chosen paths rooted in healing—one through the art of physical therapy, the power of your own words, and publishing the works of other healers; and the other through compassionate guidance, healing therapy, and the transformative language of art—and for that, I'm beyond proud. You meet others in their most vulnerable moments and help them find strength, clarity, and hope. Your work reflects a deep sensitivity to the human spirit. May your lives be filled with the same healing, love, and light you so generously offer the world.

Thank you for showing me, every day, what it means to live with grace and purpose.

All my love, always,

Mom

FOREWORD

BY DR. PAMELA J. PINE

Susan Ernst has written *Called to Serve: Standing with Survivors and Protecting Children Still at Risk,* a critical book that might just help save us all. It's both heartfelt and packed with information about human trafficking that we all need to know to engage in prevention and rescue activities. We need to work together so that the egregious act of trafficking—modern-day slavery—ends. Never doubt that this issue affects you and yours.

I am the Director of Stop the Silence®–a department of the Institute on Violence, Abuse and Trauma (IVAT). Like Sue, having come to understand the issue of, first, child sexual abuse (CSA), and its relationship to trafficking, and then other types of Adverse Childhood Experiences (or ACEs), I was drawn to do something, to make a difference, to stop the horrific abuse that affects so many girls and boys, and then the adults they become, as well as their families, communities, societies, nations, and the world in profound and terrible ways.

Child sexual and other abuse has a definitive relationship to trafficking:

- Some children experience sexual abuse or other bad aspects of home life and have no other outlets to turn to, so they go onto the street.

- Children may run away from home or stay on the street to avoid a bad home life.

- People who have been trafficked often have a difficult time understanding or providing good boundaries because of early sexual abuse.

- A pimp sees this. Pimps know how to exploit children who come from an unfortunate background. They offer them friendship, love, food, shelter, clothes, and whatever else they may want or need. In exchange, they recruit them into the commercial sex industry by manipulation, force, coercion, and deception.

There are facts we all need, like the ones above and below, to address the need, and Sue presents this type of information in an accessible and readable fashion, telling the stories of those affected, humanizing the numbers, recognizing that statistics are important, but don't tell half the story.

WE MUST TAKE NOTICE. HERE ARE SOME FACTS:

- Human trafficking is the fastest-growing means of enslavement because it has benefits for traffickers (control, money). Forced commercial sexual exploitation (alone!) generates $173 billion in illegal profits annually (ILO, 2024, https://www.ilo.org)

- There is also money made on trafficking and forced exploitation of labor in various realms.

- It's the fastest-growing international crime.

- It's one of the largest sources of income for organized crime.

- Human trafficking seems most prominent in the world's poorest countries. People are bought and sold into trafficking through fraud and the belief that they will be getting an actual job; sometimes, they are even trafficked by their own family for the money. But beware of complacency and naivety—it is happening around the U.S. and the world.

The impact of these acts cannot be understated. For the victimized people, their lived reality is one of control, deprivation, and forced depravity.

The outcomes often result in extreme negative psychological (mental health issues), physical (physical ailments, chronic disease, early death), sociological (an inability to perform well in school, difficulty getting a job, and, if gotten, to show up well for it), and economic outcomes. For our communities, these acts render us all at risk, anxious, and depleted.

For nearly 25 years, I've watched as many have tried to do something for the many millions, but, frankly, it has not been, nor will it be, enough.

I know we care about our families and communities. If we're going to reclaim safety and freedom for ourselves, children, and communities, we must learn more and be on the lookout for what is not right around us, as Sue implores. Everyone needs to learn about trafficking: the warning signs, what to do if trafficking is suspected, and who to report suspicious behavior to. And about the faces and being of those trafficked.

As such, this book is a must-read for anyone concerned about their families and communities.

Pamela J. Pine, PhD, MPH, MAIA, RCHES
Founder and Director, Stop the Silence®:
A Department of the Institute on Violence, Abuse and Trauma (IVAT)
PamelaP@ivatcenters.org Phone (cell): 240-351-7740

IVAT- Institute on Violence, Abuse and Trauma - www.ivatcenters.org
P: 858.810-6317 | F: 858.527.1743
11526 Sorrento Valley Rd, Suite A-2, San Diego, CA 92121

TABLE OF CONTENTS

INTRODUCTION | i

ABOUT THE QUOTES | v

CHAPTER 1 | 1
A CALL TO ACTION

CHAPTER 2 | 6
BE SURE YOU KNOW WHAT YOU DON'T KNOW

CHAPTER 3 | 16
ARRIVAL

CHAPTER 4 | 26
THE RESCUE FACILITY

CHAPTER 5 | 48
HEALING THROUGH PLAY

CHAPTER 6 | 58
LOVE AS A FORCE OF TRANSFORMATION

CHAPTER 7 | 66
WRITINGS FROM VOLUNTEER TEAM MEMBERS (2015-2019)

CHAPTER 8 | 89
WHAT HAPPENS AFTER RESCUE: A CLOSER LOOK

CHAPTER 9 | 93
CHALLENGES AND REFLECTIONS

CHAPTER 10 | 101
DON'T LOOK AWAY
WHEN THE MISSION IS CLOSE TO HOME

CHAPTER 11 | 110
MY PROMISE TO YOU

RESOURCES | 113

MISSION TRIP VOLUNTEER CHECKLIST | 116

READING LIST | 119

ACKNOWLEDGEMENTS | 120

ABOUT THE AUTHOR | 122

CALL TO ACTION | 124

INTRODUCTION

> "People think trafficking happens somewhere else. But it's everywhere. And it won't stop unless more people care enough to do something."
> Anonymous survivor testimony

Child sex trafficking is one of the darkest injustices of our time. It exists in every region of the world—sometimes hidden in plain sight, buried in secrecy. Behind every statistic is a child: a daughter or son, a granddaughter or grandson, a sister or brother; a life hijacked by cruelty.

I served with a team of ten volunteers at a rescue facility for children who endured exploitation or were at risk of trafficking. What we learned there speaks universally to anyone who feels called to serve. I will not name the location or the facility—doing so could put vulnerable girls at risk. While I have firsthand knowledge, some of the characters you'll read about are fictional. The stories draw on the realities found in many parts of the world. What we experienced reflects a more profound truth: trafficking is happening all over the world, and more willing hands are needed to stop it.

This book is a call to action. I speak from one place, but on behalf of many, connecting the dots between our experiences and the global mission to confront exploitation with courage, compassion, and love.

There are many perspectives when it comes to the sex trafficking of children: the child's perspective, the family's, the pedophile's, the therapist's, and the volunteer's. Certainly, there are others. This is a glimpse into one story, shared in the hope of raising awareness. Every culture, climate, and government shapes the journey differently. But the heart of the mission—to walk beside survivors with compassion and purpose—remains the same in every language, every time zone, every place of refuge.

"*Called to Serve: Standing with Survivors and Protecting Children Still at Risk* Is this book about religion?" my friend Tom asked, his voice edged with skepticism.

"No, not really. But it's about faith," I replied.

Oh boy. Here we go, I thought.

"Well, it sounds like it is. Didn't you go with a team from your church?"

"Do you have a problem with that, Tom?" I asked, a little ruffled.

"I've heard some pretty crazy stories about what happens in churches and with missionaries—some bad stuff." Tom shook his head.

"It's true that Christian individuals and organizations power much of the global anti-trafficking work. That's just the way it is—and I don't see that as a bad thing."

"Why is it mostly Christians?" Tom pressed.

Somebody has to, I thought, not without sarcasm.

"I think because Christianity calls us to 'serve the least of these.' That's compassion, Tom. Unfortunately, not all Christians live up to that call. But most do—and they do it quietly, without fanfare."

"Yeah, well, I've heard stories about missionaries going into other countries and trying to force their religion on people who aren't interested."

Why do I have to defend doing something good?

"Tom, hear me out. I've heard those stories, too. Yes, our team was grounded in Christian faith. And yes, we were there to share God's love. But not through words alone—through action, presence, and loving kindness. We weren't there to 'bring God,' as if He wasn't already there. We came to join in what was already happening—to serve, not to lead. To love, not to convert. That's the difference."

I leaned forward, hopeful. "Give it a chance, Tom. Read my story and then let's talk."

***

I'm here to say that faith—when it's rooted in humility, love, and service—can still be a force for good in this world.

Our faith was the fuel behind our compassion, not the agenda behind our mission.

You don't have to share my beliefs to read this book. You don't have to believe in God to care about justice or healing. But I hope you'll read with an open heart. I don't have all the answers—I never did—but I showed up. And this is what I saw, learned, and now carry in my soul.

Children are the embodiment of innocence, their tender hearts and open minds so vulnerable to the influences around them. From the moment they're born, they rely completely on our guidance, protection, and love. This dependence creates a sacred bond, one in which trust and security form the foundation for everything they'll become.

For children who have faced adversity, that need goes far beyond physical sustenance. They need emotional nourishment. They need to know they belong. They need to hear—over and over again—that they are seen, they matter, and they're loved.

As you turn the pages of this book, I hope you'll discover the depth of your capacity to offer hope and healing. My journey, and the journey of those I served alongside, is simply one small testament to the power of compassion—and the boundless potential within each of us to make a difference.

Let this book be a gentle guide and an honest invitation. May it inspire you to consider how your love, your gifts, and your presence might bring light into the lives of children who need it most. You don't have to have all the answers. You just have to show up with an open heart.

Together, let's embrace the mission to uplift, heal, and nurture the world's most vulnerable souls.

With love in my heart for all children,

Susan

ABOUT THE QUOTES

The chapter opening quotes throughout this book are inspired by the words and lived experiences of survivors of child sex trafficking. To protect their identities and preserve their dignity, these quotes are presented as composites—faithful to the emotional truth of survivor testimony but reworded and anonymized to avoid re-traumatization or risk of identification.

They reflect real themes, phrases, and patterns drawn from survivor interviews, advocacy reports, trauma-informed recovery programs, and trusted global anti-trafficking organizations. Every effort has been made to honor the voices of survivors with respect, compassion, and integrity.

These words are not fictional—they are echoes of what survivors around the world have courageously shared. I hope that their voices will guide and ground each chapter, reminding us of who this work is truly for.

CHAPTER 1

A CALL TO ACTION

> "I used to think no one saw me. When someone cared
> enough to show up, everything started to change."
>
> Survivor of sex trafficking

WHY I CHOSE TO VOLUNTEER

The truth is, I didn't weigh the pros and cons. There wasn't a well-reasoned "why" as much as there was a *feeling*—a deep tug in my heart. And just like that, it was a hard YES.

"Hey, buddy, I've got an idea I'd like to talk to you about," Diane said, pouring another cup of steaming coffee into her mug. She held the pot up in my direction. "Want some more?"

Diane and I met at church when my kids were teens and hers were in elementary school. Diane's family, my husband, and I attended the same church for many years.

"Cool. What's up?" I asked, holding my cup in her direction.

Over the years, our lives became deeply intertwined—first through our church, and later through our work. After a time, Diane came to work with me before hanging out her own shingle, and we've collaborated as commercial real estate appraisers for more than 25 years. Despite living far apart, we've remained close through every season of life.

"Well, I've got to give you the back story first. Got the time?" Diane asked, returning to her desk in my home office at that time.

"This sounds provocative! Okay, you have my attention," I smiled, swiveling in my office chair to face Diane, and took another sip of very strong Brazilian roast, which we fondly referred to as "lead."

"Okay. Here goes. You remember that Andy just returned from his mission trip, right?"

"Yes! That's right! How did it go?" I asked. Diane had my *full* attention now.

Andy, Diane's son, was an outgoing, cool kid with a strong faith. Andy had grown into a heart-centered young man, volunteering in various ways in third-world countries, serving vulnerable populations.

Andy had a heart for mission. The apple did not fall far from the tree. Diane was the female chaperone (and van driver), taking a group of teenagers on a mission trip to Mexico each year for fifteen years. They built houses for the impoverished, serving with teams from Amor Ministries, based in San Diego, California. Andy joined many of those trips. His passion to serve continued. Soon after graduating from high school, he served on mission trips in Haiti, Uganda, Cambodia, and Zimbabwe.

"Where are the little girls?"

Andy Blalock, Mission Trip to Uganda

When Andy went to Uganda, he met a young woman who started an orphanage for little boys. Andy served at the orphanage located in Kampala, Uganda, ministering to the boys. Shortly after his arrival, he asked the people running the orphanage, "Where are the little girls?"

They paused and said,

"They're gone. We don't have little girls here.

They were all trafficked and sold into slavery."

That was the day Andy's heart broke.

Andy's homecoming from that trip to Uganda would be the catalyst for some amazing days ahead.

"Mom, I've made a life decision. I can't sit still and do nothing. I am committing to going to those dark places in the world where girls are trafficked. I'm going to do what I can to help rescue them," Andy sat on the edge of the couch, staring at his mom's face for a reaction.

Fast forward to 2012-2013. Andy had taken a full-time position at a rescue center in a very dark corner of the world for children who were rescued from, or at risk of, sex trafficking. On one of his trips home, he told his mom about the teams that visited the rescue center where he chose to serve.

"So this is the deal. The teams come, one after another, and stay for a week or two at a time. They give the staff on-site, who live and work there 24/7, a break. Mom, I've seen what makes a good team, and I've seen what makes a bad team. I think you should bring a team over," Andy said, knowing full well what the answer would be.

It wasn't long before Diane and her sister, Karen, decided to visit the rescue facility and see for themselves.

Diane and Karen, ultimately our team's co-leaders, spent a week at the facility getting to know the staff and studying the logistics of such a trip. Upon their return to the United States, plans were put in place, and it was time to build the team.

"Mom, if you have to beg someone to join the team, they're not being called to do the work," Andy warned Diane. "Once they have your invitation, let them come to you. And watch out. One bad apple with the wrong attitude can take a team down."

Diane shared all of this with me, including Andy's work and everything she could tell me about the rescue facility. She also shared the reconnaissance mission that she and her sister, Karen, had made and their observations.

"Oh, and Sue, Andy told me one other thing," Diane said, looking at me with a sparkle in her eyes.

"Andy thinks you might be a good addition to the team. He remembers when you were his teacher in Sunday school when he was little!"

I sat in that swivel chair, holding my coffee cup with both hands. My eyes were as big as flying saucers by that time, and my heart was beating out of my chest.

"Andy told me that the primary component of our volunteering will be ministering to small children. He remembers sitting in a circle on the floor in your Sunday school class. He felt loved, safe, and happy in that circle. He thinks you'd be a good addition to the team."

Diane paused for a moment to let it sink in. "So, Karen and I are hoping you will join the team. What do you think?"

A nano-second later, jumping up from my chair, arms outstretched:

"YES!"

When Diane asked if I'd consider going, I didn't hesitate. I didn't need any more details. I didn't ask questions. I said yes *before* the questions came to mind!

So what made me think I could do this? I thought about it for a long time after I said yes.

I love kids! I want to help!

It's been a long time since I've played with little kids. Do I have what it takes?

Am I too old for this? No way! Maybe? I don't know!

What will my daughters think? Will they support me? Of course they will!

Can I afford it? I'll find a way!

God, please give me the courage, because I'm going!

Over time, many questions arose. In writing this book, I compiled a list of 29 questions that came up as we planned that first trip, and that list is tucked in the RESOURCES section.

I love kids. I love their playful spirits, honesty, and light. And when I heard this trip involved serving innocent, vulnerable children—kids who suffered more than anyone ever should—I didn't need more information. I knew I wanted to help.

I didn't go because I was brave. I went because something inside me said,

Go!

I wanted to be useful. I wanted to show up. I wanted to serve in whatever way I could.

Sometimes the most important thing you can do is say yes and trust that love will lead the way. Love was enough to push past the fear and uncertainty.

CHAPTER 2
BE SURE YOU KNOW WHAT YOU DON'T KNOW

> "People think they understand
> what we've been through.
> But unless they listen—really listen—they don't."
> Survivor of sex trafficking

I'm grateful to Dr. Pamela J. Pine for writing the foreword. Dr. Pine has presented an in-depth look at sex trafficking throughout the world. We have learned that the scale of human trafficking is staggering. It bears repeating that over 4.9 million people are currently trapped in situations of sexual exploitation worldwide, most of them women and girls. Globally, one in four victims of trafficking is a child.

I want to highlight a few other important aspects of cross-cultural ministering to understand before undergoing a mission trip.

WHY UNDERSTANDING CULTURE MATTERS
WHEN YOU VOLUNTEER ABROAD

When you show up in another country to help, it's easy to focus on what you've come to *do*. But if there's one thing I've learned, it's this: before doing anything, you must take time to understand the people and the culture you've stepped into.

You're not just stepping onto different soil—you're stepping into a whole different way of life. Things might not make sense at first. People might do things in ways that surprise you. But that's exactly why it's so important to listen, ask questions, and stay open. You're the guest. And like any good guest, it's your job to be respectful and act with humility.

The more you understand the culture, the better your chances of being helpful. Otherwise, you risk missing the mark or, even with the best of intentions, making things more complicated. But when you slow down and learn, you start to see what people need and want—not what you assume they need or want.

It also builds trust. People know when you're trying to meet them where they are. And that trust opens the door to genuine connection, real impact, and mutual respect.

Your first step? Learn everything you can about the culture you're about to visit. Read, ask questions, talk to others who've been there, and stay curious. And if you're serving vulnerable populations—like children recovering from trauma or exploitation—go even deeper. Understanding their cultural context helps you show up with the sensitivity, humility, and gentleness they deserve. You're not there to fix everything. You're there to walk beside them, for a little while, in a way that honors their story.

UNDERSTANDING COLLECTIVIST CULTURES

Look at the difference between individualist cultures and collectivist cultures. You must have this awareness as you contemplate a mission trip to a third-world country. Before volunteering at the rescue center, I read about these cultural frameworks but wasn't fully prepared for what they would mean in the context of sex trafficking. The lessons were not theoretical. They had names and faces.

Across the world, culture shapes how people see themselves, their place in a family, and their responsibilities to others. As volunteers coming from a Western mindset, we often view life through the lens of individualism. We place high value on personal freedom, choice, and self-expression. But when we step into a different culture—one that views life through a collectivist lens—our perspective is challenged in ways we never anticipated.

In **individualist cultures,** like the United States, a person's identity is largely self-defined. Success is personal. Pain is personal. And healing, we believe, is most effective when it begins with self-awareness and empowerment.

But in **collectivist cultures,** common in many parts of Asia, Africa, and Latin America, identity is deeply intertwined with the group, especially the family. In these cultures, a person's actions aren't just their own; they reflect on the entire family. Sacrifice for the good of the group is expected, and individual desires may be set aside to protect family harmony or survival.

A CHILD SOLD FOR THE SAKE OF THE FAMILY

One of the most challenging truths to face was this: some of the girls in the rescue center were sold—sometimes knowingly—by their family members.

What kind of mother or father could make such a choice?

But then I began to understand. In the most desperate corners of the world, where poverty crushes opportunity and tradition can mean sacrifice, this heartbreaking decision is sometimes seen not as betrayal, but as necessity.

Honestly, I want to understand it, but deep down, I still cannot comprehend it, but I must accept it as a reality.

In a collectivist mindset, where the needs of the family often come before those of the individual, a child might be viewed as the one who must carry the burden to ensure the survival of the whole. A daughter's body might become the family's only currency. It's horrifying. It's wrong. But within the cultural and economic reality, it may be seen as the only option.

This doesn't excuse the act—not at all. But understanding the context helped me begin to see why some girls held such complicated emotions. We, as Westerners, might expect them to feel rage. Some did. But we came to learn others held deep loyalty, even love, for those who harmed them.

They often felt shame, not because of what was done to them, but because they believed they failed their families.

THE COMPLEX PATH TO HEALING

For those who offer love, safety, and trauma-informed care, this creates a paradox. How do they help a child heal when she doesn't see herself as a victim? When all she wants is to return to the very family that sent her away? This is the case for some survivors.

Healing, in this context, cannot come through severing ties. It must come through reframing identity—helping her see herself not just as a daughter or sister but as a whole and worthy human being—someone with value beyond what she can offer others.

Please remember that although the victims are mostly girls, boys are trafficked too and must not be forgotten in this fight.

That takes patience, cultural humility, and grace. And all of this takes time, perhaps decades.

WHAT THIS CULTURE TAUGHT ME

This experience showed me that healing does not look the same in every culture. It also taught me to stop assuming that my way (my values and beliefs about right and wrong) is the only lens through which to interpret the world.

On the other hand, it also confirmed something unshakable: every child deserves to be protected. Every girl or boy has the right to safety, dignity, and joy, regardless of what their culture has told them, regardless of what their family has done.

Consistent, nonjudgmental love transcends cultures. And when it does, something extraordinary can happen. We begin to see the child not only as a survivor, but as someone rising, someone remembering who she is, not who she was told to be. But understandably, this is not always the case. And that's when I lean on prayer and hope.

CAN YOU EVER BE FULLY PREPARED?

As the van bounced its way around the final corner, the narrow road ahead shimmered with heat and dust. On the roadside, a group of older men lounged around a battered metal picnic table, the kind that looked like it had been forgotten by time. A sun-bleached umbrella, torn and sagging, offered little relief from the blistering sun. Smoke curled lazily from half-lit cigarettes clinging to their lips, their eyes following the van for a heartbeat before drifting away, blank and unreadable.

They didn't flinch. They didn't smile. They didn't care.

Or maybe they cared too much. Maybe that wasn't apathy I saw—maybe it was something colder. Contempt? Disdain? I felt a shiver crawl up my spine.

I scanned my teammates. *Was anyone else watching them? Sensing the same uneasy shift in the air?*

I nudged my seatmate. "Those guys…" I whispered. "Do they seem off to you?"

She didn't meet my eyes. "Yes, ugh," she replied in a low voice, eyes fixed on the opposite window.

I turned my face back toward the glass, heat turning my cheeks bright red. Shame turned to acid, burning a hole in my stomach.

I don't know them. I know nothing about them. And already, I'm judging them. Good grief. Get a grip!

Here I was, writing a story in my head—one shaped by the darkest things I'd read before I ever got here.

Great job, Susan. Way to start suspecting every man you see.

Sweat beaded on my upper lip. The guilt was instant. And it was heavy.

We were a block away. After months of planning and an incredibly long trip, we were a block away from the beginning of an experience I will never forget.

We're one block from the children we flew across the world to meet. One block from the answers to all the questions we didn't dare to ask out loud.

This was it. "Pull yourself together," I mumbled to myself and sat up straight on the worn leather seat. Bam! The van hit a large pothole, dust flying, and we all bounced off our seats, barely missing the roof of the van.

Nothing would ever be the same.

WHY THIS MATTERS—AND WHY I WROTE THIS BOOK

I don't have the perfect words for what I saw or felt when serving at a rescue facility for children at risk of exploitation. People talk about numbers, laws, and global efforts—and yes, those things matter. But they don't even come close to what it's like to sit with a child who's learning to feel safe again. They don't show you the moment a little girl, who once believed she had no worth, starts to laugh. Or the quiet miracle of a child slipping their hand into yours—not because they have to, but because they want to. I carry their faces with me. The way they looked at us—sometimes curious, sometimes shy, sometimes with no light in their eyes, and sometimes full of hope—and how they let us in. No statistics in the world can explain that. But once you've felt it, you're never the same.

That's why I called these trips life-changing and why I wrote this book.

I'm not a social worker. I'm not a therapist. I am a volunteer. Over five years, our team spent ten days each year at a rescue facility that serves girls and boys rescued from trafficking and children at risk of being trafficked. I witnessed not only the heartbreaking wounds of exploitation but also the breathtaking resilience of children healing through trust, love, and play.

There's much that is broken in this world. But there is also much that can be mended. I hope that by sharing what I've seen and learned, others will be moved to serve—not from a place of pity, but from the deep belief that every child is worthy of safety, dignity, and joy.

In the chapters that follow, I invite you to experience a place that forever changed my life. You'll meet children whose stories have stayed with me (and the team) long after we returned home, and volunteers whose presence helped bring light back into the lives of those they served. The team offers reflections and practical guidance for when you're called to step into this work yourself.

More than anything, this is a story of hope—and of the quiet, faithful ways that love can begin to heal even the deepest wounds.

ELENA'S STORY PART ONE
(A fictional tale built on reality)

CONTENT WARNING:

**This chapter contains depictions of child trafficking, including familial betrayal and exploitation.
Reader discretion is advised.**

AND NOW IMAGINE...

Mia stepped to the edge of the old wooden dock, bare feet gripping the sun-warmed planks. One hand shaded her eyes as she scanned past the river's mouth toward the vast blue sweep of ocean. The dock creaked and shifted beneath her weight, bobbing gently in rhythm with her rising anxiety.

A mosquito landed on her arm—*slap*—gone. She didn't even look. Her gaze stayed locked on the choppy water. The sea was rough.

From here, the fishing boats looked like toys, rocking and dipping, some nearly swallowed by the waves.

"Where is he?" she whispered, heart pounding. "He's been gone since dawn."

She clasped her hands tight and lifted her face to the sky, pleading silently. *Please. Let this be his lucky day.* The prayer was more desperate than hopeful.

The stench of rotting garbage hung heavily in the humid air, wafting from a mound at the far end of the dock. Mia winced, turned away, and retreated toward the patchwork shack she called home—scraps of sheet metal and splintered wood barely holding together.

She pulled aside the worn mosquito netting and peered in. Her son and daughter lay curled together on the thin, stained mattress in the corner—their family bed. A single beam of light filtered through a crack in the wall, landing on her daughter's face. So still. So peaceful.

Mia froze. Her throat tightened. *Why couldn't she have been a boy?*

The thought hit her like a slap. She sank to her knees and buried her face in her hands—shame, grief, guilt—all of it pressed down at once.

Mia rummaged through the upturned cardboard box she used as a shelf, even though she already knew—she'd seen the emptiness last night, just before collapsing beside her children on the frayed sheet that passed for their bed. It hadn't magically filled itself overnight.

Beside the cold cooking pot, a crumpled burlap sack lay in a heap. Still, she gave it a shake, hoping for a miracle. A few lone grains of rice slipped into the pot. Not enough to feed a rat, let alone her four-year-old son or her twelve-year-old daughter.

She lowered herself onto the three-legged stool, her legs trembling, and poked at the fire with a long-handled spoon. Her eyes burned—not just from the smoke.

Boiled water for breakfast. Again.

She reached for a small pouch and pinched in a few tea leaves. One more stir. One more morning.

The fishing was poor that season. No one knew why. Day after day, the men pushed their boats farther out to sea, chasing hope across the waves, only to return with empty nets and hollow faces. Whatever they caught was split among too many hands, leaving barely enough to show for it.

Mia turned back to the pot, glancing once more at her sleeping children. A familiar panic began to crawl up her spine.

"I must do something," she whispered, her hands trembling.

Her forehead beaded with sweat. She wiped it away, scanning the room as if an answer might appear in the thin air.

"Please, God—let there be fish today." The words escaped in a gasp. The walls seemed to close in. Her husband's foot looked worse this morning—angry and red with infection. She knew he'd never see a doctor. There was no money for that.

Mia pressed her hands to the sides of her head, trying to silence the racing thoughts. She sat. Stood. Sat again.

Her hand flew to her cheek. Another tooth ached—throbbed.
If I lose another tooth...I can't go to the dentist.
Paralyzed, she stood there, frozen by the weight of it all.

If something didn't change soon, they'd have to work the fields. All of them. Even the children.

She thought of her sister—of her niece and nephew, faces drawn, eyes bloodshot, arms covered in raw, cracked cuts from long days under the brutal sun.

Mia had seen enough. She knew exactly what that life would cost.

Mia slumped onto the stool and buried her face in her hands. Tears streamed down her flushed cheeks, soaking into her palms. From the corner, a soft whimper broke the silence—her son, stirring. The sound made her stomach clench. Soon, he would cry. He would beg for food.

She wiped her face quickly with the hem of her skirt, forcing herself to stay quiet, to stay strong.

"Hello! Anyone in there?"

The deep voice cut through the thick air like a blade. Mia jolted, her heart leaping into her throat. She turned toward the opening in the wall, blinking against the sudden shaft of sunlight. A tall man stood outside, one hand braced on the sagging roof as he bent to peer inside. His face was hidden in shadow.

"Yes?" Mia answered, her voice barely above a whisper. She stepped back instinctively.

The man smiled. "Does Elena live here?"

Mia's breath caught.

"This is your lucky day," he said. "I've come to offer your daughter a great job in the city. I'll give you three hundred dollars now. There'll be more later."

Story to be continued in a later chapter.

CHAPTER 3

ARRIVAL

> "You don't have to be perfect.
> Just being there told me I mattered."
> Survivor of sex trafficking

AT LAST

We shared a devotion as we drove to the rescue facility each morning. This grounded us and set the tone for the frame of mind we carried throughout that day. On occasion, this triggered pent-up tears, and that was a good thing, but more often than not, we were filled with anticipation and excitement.

"Hope we have enough crafts!" a teammate called from the back of the van.

"We've got plenty. I made extra. But all hands on deck, okay? This first one is going to involve stringing beads," Cindy called out, laughing. We had been warned about how hard it was for tiny hands to do what we thought was so easy.

"Hey, I'm working with the counselors today and won't be able to help," Karen said, glancing up from her planning binder.

"Me too," Deb called out, sitting next to Karen, both flipping through paperwork.

"No worries, we've got plenty of folks. We've got this!" I said.

"Yeah, we can make sure that there is a teen in each small group to help the little guys," Margie added.

"Hey, Diane, you're going to join me for self-defense class, right?" Meg called from the back of the van.

"Yep! I'll be there. Hey guys, don't forget, we're going to deliver rice to some families today before lunch period," Diane responded, turning to face us all from the front seat.

"We're almost there, guys. Let's pray." John opened up his binder to the first page.

A Thanksgiving Prayer
Commonly attributed to Samuel F. Pugh

O God,

When I have food, help me to remember the hungry.

When I have work, help me to remember the jobless.

When I have a warm home, help me to remember the homeless.

When I am without pain, help me to remember those who suffer.

And remembering,
help me to destroy my complacency and bestir my compassion.

Make me concerned enough to help, by word and deed,
those who cry out for what we take for granted.

The van carrying our team finally pulled over and came to a stop in front of a weathered, three-story building—its concrete exterior chipped and cracked, its wooden frame sagging from years of heat and humidity. As the driver turned off the engine, an uneasy silence settled over us. The hum of the motor was replaced by the sudden stillness of a foreign place now very real. The van doors swung open, and the thick, humid air rushed in like a wave. It was stifling, heavy with the sour stench of sewage rising from nearby drains, mingled with the unexpected sharpness of frying garlic wafting from somewhere nearby. The contrast was jarring, grounding us in the truth of where we were. We had arrived.

The front of the building was nondescript with no signage; its purpose was revealed by the throng of bedraggled but happy children standing at the front doorway, all eyes on our van.

My heart pounded triple time, not just with nerves, but with something more profound, wild, open-hearted expectation. I had no idea what I was about to walk into, only that it mattered. It mattered *deeply*.

A dozen or so kids, ranging in age from tiny to teens, were there to greet us, standing in the haze of a bright sun. Several older women sat on the dusty ground nearby, some of them holding babies. Did I mention it was hot and humid—oppressively so, but the kids wore the weather like it was their favorite sweater. Their beautiful brown skin glistened in the sun as they stood barefoot or in flip-flops, hand-me-down clothes clinging to their bodies with sweat and dust. Their faces were smeared with dirt, their hair tangled, and their feet were filthy. And yet—*they beamed.*

Oh, my goodness, they are so precious!

I can't believe it! We're here!

This is really happening!

Big brown eyes, full of joy, intent on who was about to climb out of that van. Their bright smiles instantly transported their happiness to each member of the team. The kids didn't know us yet, but it seemed they were convinced we came to be with them and that they were safe. In their world, that was more than enough. This was not their first rodeo. But it sure was ours.

Diane turned around in the front seat and looked back at me. Our eyes met— glistening, full of tears. In unison, we both brought our hands to our chests, sharing in the excitement of that moment.

We hadn't even left the van, and I knew: *I will never be the same.*

We scrambled out of the van into a tangled mess of outstretched arms. The children ran toward us with radical trust, wrapped their arms around our waists, grabbed our hands, and pulled us into their world. Some of them learned all about "high-fives" and held their little hands up to anyone who'd return the slap. It was loud and chaotic. It was pure joy. Within seconds, a tiny, sticky hand grabbed my hand, and I brushed back sweat-soaked bangs from a little forehead with the other.

"Hi! Hello!" We all called out in the children's language, spinning around, quickly surrounded by girls and boys clamoring to meet us. So far, we hadn't done anything to earn this love-fest. It was incredibly humbling.

I still can't quite put words to what I felt in that moment. But this is close:

Chaos everywhere—kids laughing, jumping, pulling at our hands, our hearts. We're hugging them back, all of us, swallowed up in joy. And yet… in the middle of it, I feel it. A quiet holiness.

Love holds us in its wide embrace. Somehow, even in all this noise, we're wrapped in something sacred.

I didn't know what else to say to the kids, but I suppose the wide grin plastered on my face told the story. I had no clue how this would go, but any lingering worries began to dissolve.

I'm here. It's enough.

In that instant, I began to understand something that would shape every moment that followed: the simple, sacred power of showing up.

THE POWER OF SHOWING UP

I had no formal training in trauma care. What I *had* was a willing heart, ten days to give, and a quiet sense that simply being there, really being there, mattered more than I understood at the time.

Who am I to walk into a place where children were potentially healing from unthinkable trauma? What can I possibly offer?

But as I sat on the floor with my teammates and we played a simple clapping game with dozens of our new best friends vying for seats next to us—some wary, mostly curious—I began to understand: *presence is a gift.*

There's something sacred about showing up, especially in a world where so many people turn away. When we step into painful places, not with solutions but with open hearts, we offer something rare. We say:

> **"You matter. Your life matters. You are not forgotten."**

USING OUR GIFTS IN SERVICE TO OTHERS

When it came to building our team, sacred work was at hand. I've never seen such a perfect blend of talents and personalities, all united by one common thread: to serve those kids in the best way we knew how, knowing that God would guide us.

We were all in the same proverbial boat: Few of us had traveled to this country before. Most of us hadn't volunteered for a service project of this scale before. Each of us had fears and concerns about our effectiveness, and possibly, our safety. And thankfully, all of us love kids, and backed by our faith, we wanted to do this with all our hearts.

I recall one essential tool all teams must remember: compassion for one another. Although our spirits were high most days, we were frequently reminded of the fragile hearts masked by those smiling faces. Some experiences brought us to our knees. As a team, we recognized when a member needed to step away to shed a few tears or get some air, and that vigilance kept us whole. Always on the lookout, one member stepped up to take the place of another; no questions asked.

AN UNBROKEN CHAIN

"You will be blessed by them," is what everyone told us.

In the van on our way to the rescue center, on the first day:

"Did you say there will be like 90 to 125 kids there?" One of us asked.

"That's right," Diane yelled over the noise of the engine from one of the front seats. "They're never sure exactly how many kids will show up each day."

"And these little kids can't speak English, right?" another teammate yelled toward the front of the van.

"That's right," Karen replied, turning around in her seat to face the rest of us.

"So, how, exactly, are we going to be a blessing to these kids?" Another teammate asked a question I'm sure most of us were thinking at that point.

It wasn't long before we had an answer to that question, and it's a lesson none of us will forget.

On our first day, the facility's pastor gathered the volunteer team, local counselors, and social workers. He spoke fluidly in both his native language and English, and his eyes gleamed with the wisdom of experience and compassion.

"These children have nothing. They have no hope. They have no love. They have nothing. All we ask is that you 'pour love on' these kids. Play with them. Give them a reason to hope."

At that moment, I understood how this might work. We brought them new faces to brighten their days, fresh songs to lift their spirits, and new games to spark joy. More importantly, we offered them an unbroken chain of love, hope, and safety. We hoped they could trust these humans and, in turn, share that trust among themselves. We hoped their generation might grow up with just a glimmer of hope, loving kindness, and a reason to make their world a better place.

ELENA'S STORY PART TWO
(A fictional tale based on reality)

CONTENT WARNING:

This chapter contains depictions of child trafficking, including familial betrayal and exploitation. Reader discretion is advised.

AND NOW IMAGINE THIS...

The fast-moving car bounced hard as it hit a pothole in the pavement, jerking Elena out of a drugged sleep. Her body bounced, and her head snapped to the side.

Her heart beat out of her chest. Her skin stuck to the leather seat as she pushed herself up just enough to see the driver, a man with short, brown hair. She caught a glimpse of his clammy, pale face in the rearview mirror. Huge sunglasses masked his eyes; his mouth was a thin, colorless line.

Elena dropped back down on the seat, both hands clamped over her mouth to stifle a scream building up from deep inside.

She had never been in a car before.

A wave of dizziness swept over her.

Mama?

Mama!

Where are you? MAMA!

She screamed, but no sound left her lips.

Who is this man?

Where is he taking me?

What happened to me?

She rubbed her forehead as a massive headache took hold. Elena tried to open the locked car door, slumped back onto the seat, and the darkness swallowed her again.

"Take her into the room at the end of the hall," a woman's voice whispered quickly, slamming the door behind them. Elena felt massive arms squeezing tighter. The smell of cigarette smoke permeated the air.

What was that noise?

Is that a child crying? A loud slap. The crying stops.

Where am I?

Elena swallowed, fighting the bile making its way up her throat. She lost consciousness again.

The cold cement floor jolted Elena awake, and she sat up too quickly, dizziness forcing her to catch herself with both hands. The small room, no larger than a closet, was pitch-black. There were no windows. As her eyes grew accustomed to the blackness, shadows became shapes, and for the first time, she saw a small wooden cot in one corner of the room.

Gathering all her strength, Elena crawled to the cot and, holding onto the top of it, pulled herself up and collapsed. A wave of nausea came and went as she clamped her mouth shut in defiance.

After a few minutes, she took a deep breath, stood up, and, trembling, crossed the floor to the door. Holding one hand with the other to stop the shaking, she turned the handle carefully to avoid making noise, realized it was locked, and returned to the cot. Pushing the cot against one wall, she curled into a ball and tried to disappear. Her tears formed a small puddle on the rough canvas as she drifted into a feverish sleep.

It must have been hours—maybe days—no windows, no light.

Oh God, where am I?

Elena sat on the edge of the cot, her long hair clinging to her damp face. She pulled it back with trembling fingers, tucking strands behind her ears as she licked her dry, cracked lips.

I'm so thirsty. How long have I been here?

She scanned the corners of the room. Nothing. No windows. No furniture, just the cot beneath her. Her stomach twisted.

I need to pee.

Her hands began to shake. Tears slid down her cheeks without sound. She wrapped her arms around herself and rocked gently, back and forth, trying not to fall apart.

Mama…please…where are you?

A door creaked open somewhere beyond her room. Elena froze. Laughter. Voices—loud, slurred, clinking glasses. Music thumping faintly. Then, the door slammed shut. Silence.

Her breath caught as footsteps approached. Each step sent a wave of nausea through her. Cigarette smoke drifted in under the door.

The key turned in the lock.

Metal on metal.

The knob twisted.

The door opened just an inch.

Elena stared, paralyzed.

A woman's thin, brown arm reached through the gap, pushing a bowl of gray mush across the floor. A plastic water bottle followed—tossed carelessly. It landed near the cot with a thud.

Next came an empty tin can. Then a filthy rag. The door shut. The lock turned. Gone.

Silence again.

Time blurred. Later—how much later, she couldn't tell—the door squeaked again and slammed shut.

Voices. Men, this time. Deep, indistinct. Footsteps. Heavy ones.

The key turned. The knob began to move.

Elena backed up, pressing her spine to the wall. Her arms wrapped tightly around her ribs. Knees pulled to her chest. Her body shook so hard it felt like her bones might rattle.

The handle turned slowly.

Evil was at the door.

"Please help me," she whispered into the darkness.

Two years passed.

Story to be continued in a later chapter.

CHAPTER 4
THE RESCUE FACILITY

> "That place became my first safe memory."
> Survivor of sex trafficking

SACRED GROUND

They told us that every building of their facility used to be a brothel that sold children, some as young as eight.

I didn't think that a decrepit building, rebuilt with fresh paint and hope, could feel so holy, but as we climbed to the third floor and sat on the edge of that wooden stage, something told me this was sacred ground.

We were ten close friends bonded together over months of planning, praying, and preparation for this mission. We packed suitcases with supplies and hearts full of hope, and yet, in that moment, we heard the approaching footsteps of children whose lives knew more hardships than we could imagine.

Are we truly ready for this? I'm guessing I wasn't the only one asking that question.

We heard the sound of many flip-flops slapping the concrete floor below us as the kids raced for the stairwell. We exchanged wide-eyed looks and broad smiles. I swiped at a bead of sweat that made its way down the side of my face, quickly pulled out my water bottle from my back pocket, and took a gulp.

The stairwell filled with the thunder of small feet, hooting and hollering. The large double doors burst open, and two older kids secured each side as the younger kids ran in. They came in waves, arms outstretched, faces lit up with something between curiosity and joy.

Dressed for play, they all wore mismatched shorts and well-worn T-shirts. A few had pajamas on. As the kids moved closer to check out one of our guy's hairy legs or to get a close-up of those mesmerizing blue eyes for the first time, the smell of sweat and, occasionally, a hint of pee was in the air.

The shy kids or those who appeared frightened, uncomfortable, or depressed were easy to spot. Initially, it was hard to know exactly what was wrong, but it was easy to see that something wasn't right. I believe each of us was making mental notes to seek out each of those who needed a little extra help.

A little girl took me by surprise and launched herself into my lap without hesitation. I wrapped my arms around her waist so she wouldn't fall off. Her bright brown eyes glistened as she stared intently into my eyes, and, looking quite serious, she tried to touch my eye with a tiny pointer finger.

"Hi, my name is Susan! How – are – you – today?" I said slowly. She didn't speak but gave me a big smile.

I gave her a hug and turned her around, so she sat facing the kids on the floor. I ignored the sweat forming between her little bare legs and my lap. All that was left was love, pure, uncomplicated, and immediate. We both were content; no talking was necessary at this point. The togetherness seemed to be all that was needed.

Several older kids were the last to arrive and closed the doors behind them. They looked tired, and by the flat expression on their faces, I'm guessing that their patience dissolved hours earlier. Try corralling 90 to 125 kids each day! *Every day.* We grew to love those kids. Most of them called this place home. The younger kids knew that this handful of teens was "boss."

The teens joined us each day and helped maintain some sense of orderly chaos as we led the kids through our planned games, crafts, puppet shows, dancing, and other activities. A couple of the older kids acted as our interpreters, explaining the steps of a craft project or the rules of the game we were about to play in the children's native language. Over time, we built a special bond with the older kids, and they began to share more and more with us. I am reminded that due to the language barrier, it was important to watch for the little moments that reflected so much.

We were about three or four days into our trip. This morning, we were having trouble getting the kids to line up for our next game. Several of the little boys were horsing around, and no matter what I tried, they wouldn't settle down. I looked at my teen interpreter, and I'm guessing my eyes reflected exasperation. She nodded and smiled at me. Suddenly, she stood up, clapped her hands firmly, said something very firmly in her native language, and all the kids plopped down on the floor, one behind the other, in perfect formation, hands folded in their laps. We both smiled at each other and, with a new understanding, bowed to each other; me, in gratitude.

I believe that up until that moment, she had been trying to give me and the other teammates full rein, as a sign of respect. But, thankfully, she recognized that it was time to help us out, and she learned that we respected her equally. The beauty in this was that no words were necessary.

I glanced over at my teammates on the stage—each one of them already wrapped up in a sea of little brown hands and bright smiles. One knelt to pick up a particularly small boy and sat him down on the stage with an arm around his tiny shoulders. Another clumsily mimicked a little girl's silly dance to her delight. Another had her arms full as several of the older girls competed for a spot on her lap.

Each team member had a distinct personality and skills. Some of us were older, others younger. Some loved to sing or dance; others preferred sitting with a shy child and playing quietly. A few of us loved to ham it up for our plays and puppet shows, and others were happy behind the scenes. The children were not picky about who they played with. They weren't looking for perfect people. They were looking for presence. And *that,* we all gave, with love.

Once all the kids were settled on the dusty floor, I greeted them. Forcing tears of excitement back, I smiled at them all and said,

"Good morning! My name is Susan," I greeted the kids, placing my hand on my heart, which was beating, once again, triple time.

I turned to the teen sitting next to me on the stage and, holding my palm up in her direction, signaled for her to interpret what I said.

"Good morning! My name is *Suusaan,*" our wonderful teen mimicked me with a broad smile on her face, and the kids all laughed.

"We are so happy to be here!" I said, trying to take in every sweet face looking up at me and my teammates in excited anticipation.

"We are so happy to be here!" my interpreter repeated, in their language, smiling and holding her arms out in an exaggerated stretch. Once again, laughter from every corner of the room.

"These are my teammates," I gestured to the team. We stood up, and as I called out each teammate's name, they offered a greeting to the kids in the kids' native language, which the team had practiced ahead of time.

At this point, our teen helpers lined up the kids in ten or so rows, sometimes forming lines of girls and lines of boys, and sometimes in special groups that only they understood.

This is where things started to get crazy for the team and funny for the kids. The teens led us in memorable songs, dances, and exercise routines, and our team did everything we could to quickly learn the steps or sing along, sometimes to our embarrassment, but always to the kids' delight. In hindsight, I realize the teens were trying to wear the little kids out so that the rest of the day would go a little smoother. Meanwhile, we tried to keep up. The little kids could've gone on like that for hours!

While some of us danced and sang with the kids, a few retreated to prepare for whatever was up next on the schedule. When keeping 100 kids busy, preparation was the key, and we got good at it!

Each day's schedule included:

Morning: Special programs for older youth, such as bible studies, help with reading, self-defense classes, and computer classes, were offered each year, depending on the composition of our team and their skill sets.

Afternoon:

- Skit or Puppet Show

- Game

- Craft

- Song/Dance led by the teens

I never stopped being amazed at the healing power of simple things: offering a helping hand to a small child determined to string those beads with her tiny fingers; teammates dancing like goofballs, throwing dignity out the window, encouraging the little ones, especially those less brave, to join in. These weren't grand gestures. They were small, ordinary acts of love—and they held extraordinary weight.

Showing up is not about fixing. It's about being. It's about saying with your presence,

I see you. I won't run from your pain. I will stay for as long as I can and hold space with you.

OVERWHELM, AWE, AND JOY

I admit, initially, I felt completely overwhelmed. There were so many of them—tiny, steamy bodies moving in all directions, laughter bouncing off the walls, sticky little hands reaching, grabbing, hugging, and tugging.

I tried to keep up, smile at each face, and let them know they were loved. I wanted to do this perfectly.

Susan, they aren't looking for perfection!

The noise was like a wave, and I was caught in it—delighted, dizzy, and barely able to process the sheer *volume* of kid energy coming at me.

As I knelt to greet one child, I looked around and finally saw them—dusty feet, worn-out clothes, hair tangled by their raucous play, and sweaty faces lit up with joy. These children had every reason to retreat, harden, and protect themselves—but instead, they ran toward love like they had never been denied it.

How does someone who has experienced abuse and neglect still smile like that? Still trust?

These are the questions that stopped me in my tracks. I saw a child's eyes light up, hand reaching for mine, laughter bubbling up from some deep place inside—and wondered: *How? How is it possible that after everything, there's still joy? Still hope?*

It defies logic. But maybe that's the point.

Their apparent resilience doesn't come from being untouched by pain. It comes from surviving it, from someone showing up, from one safe adult, from a thousand small kindnesses that begin to rewrite the story.

They smile because deep down, they *want* to believe in good. I believe they trust again because they *need* to believe love is real. Just as I do. I was taught that God is love. I was taught that we should love one another. And when we show up—again and again—we help make that belief possible.

That smile? It's not a miracle. It's a choice they've made, again and again, to keep their heart open.

And it teaches us more than we could ever teach them.

***

And just like that, one little boy wrapped his arms around my waist and looked up at me with total certainty, like he'd known me forever. In that moment, every fear I brought with me—every doubt about being good enough, strong enough, worthy enough—melted away.

All that was left was joy.

Pure, uncomplicated, sacred joy.

And the knowing that I was exactly where I was meant to be.

A LOT TO LEARN

A pile of flip-flops at the entrance to the playroom marks the beginning of another magical day.

We greet the kids in their native language—it means, "Hi, how are you?" We've practiced for weeks.

They respond instantly with a similar greeting and begin the search for their new, temporary soulmates. They know. They've done this week after week because, thankfully, teams from all over the world come to this place every few weeks or so to offer their help to the most incredible team that lives here permanently and dedicates their lives to this work.

The children know they're safe here, and that these people, who look so different from them, are good and here to love them, even if it's for a brief time. And they are hungry for that love.

How am I supposed to say goodbye next week?
I love them already!
Every one of them!

But this is just the second day. I have a lot to learn.

And there he is again, my little guy. He runs up to me and puts his hand out to high-five me. I'm guessing he's about six or seven years old. I'm not sure. The kids are small for their age, often due to poor nutrition. The kids learned this Americanized greeting. I patted his hand and let him slap the palm of my hand. He looks into my eyes. The twinkle in his eye tells me that he's curious about this white lady with blue eyes.

His eyes are big and brown.

What have those beautiful eyes seen? I wonder as I stare back, smile so wide my cheeks hurt.

His little mouth is a bit disfigured. Looks like a cleft palate and a rough repair job. Tiny teeth appear in the most endearing smile I've ever seen, and my heart breaks.

His T-shirt and shorts are filthy and smell of sweat, dirt, and pee. Wanting to hug him, instead, I offer up another high five.

He can't speak English, and I can't speak his language, except for a few words of greeting, so I continue to speak to him in English, keeping my voice soft and body relaxed so that he will know how happy I am to meet him. He seems comfortable with this and continues to smile at me.

"My name is Susan," I say, patting my chest with one hand. "What is your name?" I extend my hand out towards him. He doesn't respond but pokes my chin with a tiny finger and laughs.

Not exactly sure what I should do next, I crouch down and start counting his fingers. "One, two, three. . ." as I touch the tip of each finger with my pointer finger. He watches intently as I make my way to his other hand. "Ten!" I look up at him and smile. He smiles back and points at one of my fingers. I say "One!" and he mimics me. "One!"

We make our way to "Ten!" and I throw my hands in the air and shout "Yahoooo!" It's one of those moments I will never forget. On our first day, we found a way to bond. No language barrier here!

Each day, I seek him out in the crowd, and a dozen times or more, our eyes meet across the room, and we both smile and wave. When it's time for the older kids to lead us in a song or dance, he waves at me and belly laughs as he watches me happily making a fool of myself.

On the third day, I searched the room but couldn't find him. He was nowhere to be seen. My heart raced.

Each day, our team left the rescue facility during our lunch break, climbed into the van, and drove into the surrounding area. Accompanied by staff from the rescue facility, we delivered 20-pound sacks of rice to impoverished families. The team purchased the rice from a local farmer beforehand, coordinated by the rescue facility. It's a fact that one sack of rice might be enough to prevent a child from being sold into trafficking.

The families we saw live in patchwork huts made from scraps of cardboard, sheet metal, and whatever else they can find. The huts are small, with one room at best, and there are no toilets.

On the fourth day, I ran to Diane. "I found him!" I said, fighting back tears. We hugged each other with relief.

He was sitting with his family on a plastic tarp on the ground under an awning shaded from the hot sun as they received our greeting, prayers, and, thankfully, the rice.

He smiled and waved, and I waved back at the same time, hopping from one foot to the other to shake biting ants off my feet. It took everything in me not to run up to him, wrap him up in my arms, and run away!

After we distributed the rice, some of us walked with the families to their homes and got a glimpse of their everyday lives. I watched my new little friend disappear into a doorless opening on the side of a decrepit lean-to. I climbed into the van with the rest of the team and, finding a seat at the back, I let the tears fall.

***

On the last day of that week, the team stood in a single-file line and greeted each child with a high-five as they left for the day. The little kids came first, yelling and running. The older kids walked at a slower pace. We all had tears in our eyes. They knew, and we knew—we might not ever see each other again.

I took a few slow breaths as the emotion of this moment took hold. I felt like I had a vice around my heart, and I knew I wasn't the only one.

This is even harder than I thought it would be, I thought, wishing I could sit down. I remember squeezing my teammate's arm, and she squeezed back.

My little guy came up and wrapped his arms around my legs. I leaned down to return his hug. We made butterflies that day, and he proudly pushed his butterfly into my hands, gesturing that I should keep it. He painted it completely black. It looks like a bat, not a butterfly. I will treasure it always. In fact, it adorns the cover of this book. I held it in the palm of my hands and, looking down, I mumbled, "God bless you," as I wiped sweat and tears from my eyes with my shirt sleeve.

One last smile, one more high-five, and he ran to another newly found soulmate to say his goodbyes.

Each member of our team has stories like this—dozens of stories. Every evening, we sat at our communal table back at the hotel and shared those stories. We laughed and cried.

END OF DAY

We gave out our last high-fives and wrapped as many little bodies into our arms as we could, whispering, "See you tomorrow," repeatedly. And we meant it. Each promise felt like a thread—thin but strong—woven between us and them.

Just like that, they were gone. The stairwell echoed with their fading footsteps, and the room exhaled a sigh. The silence left behind was startling, almost sacred. Where there was laughter and music and squeals and chaos, now there was stillness except for the *whoosh, whoosh* of the overhead fans. Scraps of paper, ribbon, or glitter carpeted the wood floor. A pair of flip-flops lay forgotten near the door. A few partially finished water bottles rested on the windowsills or on the stage where volunteers had left them. Sunlight filtered in through the windows, casting long shadows across the sticky wooden floor where just moments before, so many stories unfolded.

TEAM DEBRIEF

We looked at each other—tired, soaked in sweat, completely wrung out—and smiled. There was a quiet understanding between us:

Something extraordinary happened in that room. And it will happen again tomorrow.

After the last child disappeared down the stairs, we all lingered for a moment in that echo of silence, letting our hearts catch up to the day.

We were exhausted, sticky with sweat, and emotionally drained, so a complete debrief wouldn't happen until later, after we returned to our hotel and dinner hour.

CLEANUP

I think if any of us sat down at that point, we wouldn't be able to get up. Okay, who am I kidding? Speak for yourself, old woman! *You're almost there!*

A few of us grabbed brooms from a stack leaning against the wall at the back of the room. Others dismantled our stage props and put away chairs and other miscellaneous items used for our games and crafts. Working together, we swept up all the scraps left behind.

Secret just for you, reader: I liked the sweeping part because I could do that standing up, holding the broom like a long cane. After hours of bending over, crouching, bending, sitting on a wooden floor, did I say bending? Well, you get it!

We bagged the trash and tied it up, mopped where needed, and cleaned with care. This special place deserved to be cared for, and it was one thing we could do for the on-site teen volunteers while we were there.

We mainly worked in silence now, in that good kind of tiredness, the kind that comes after giving everything you have to something that matters. Finished, we collected our leftover supplies, water bottles, and daily plan binders and headed downstairs to our waiting van.

REFLECTIONS

As I open the door to my hotel room, a blast of cool air greets me. I kick off my flip flops, plop down on the edge of my bed, and take a breath. Too tired to speak, but my heart is so full of things to say. I lie back on the cool sheets and stare at the ceiling.

I know I'm exactly where I'm meant to be.

To be part of something this good—so purely good—it feels like such a privilege. And such a responsibility.

My heart—it's split wide open. Not empty. No, not empty at all. It's stretching, somehow, making space for more love than I ever thought I could hold.

These children laugh, after everything—they laugh, they're so brave, they seem to shine with joy. In just one day, they've carved themselves into me. I carry them now. My God, this is humbling.

Will I be enough for them?

Will I have the strength, the patience, the energy to give them all I can?

I don't want to let them down. God, help me do this right.

Thank you for this team—we need each other. And together, maybe we can give these kids what they deserve most: love that never fails them.

It healed me, too, though I didn't know yet all the ways it would. Something in me softened. Something in me awakened. I came to serve and give, but what I received was beyond anything I imagined—love, so simple, fierce, and freely given.

Eventually, I peeled off the soggy layers of the day and stepped into the small, tiled shower—glorious hot water, a precious gift, washing away the dust and raw emotion clinging to me.

Refreshed, I met the team downstairs for dinner. These were some of my favorite times, where exhaustion turned to renewed energy, and laughter filled the space between bites of delicious food. We found a second wind around those tables. We shared stories, replayed funny moments, and held space for the tender ones, all while quietly holding back the heavier things we couldn't quite say out loud yet.

"Oh my God, the older kids were such a blast today! Total goofballs," I said, taking a welcome sip of iced tea laced with fresh mint. The cold glass felt good in my hand after the heat of the day.

"Did you see their faces when we wrapped Jordan in balloons and let them tackle him to pop them?" John laughed, lifting a cold glass of beer and taking a sip. "That was hysterical! They play rough!" His laugh carried easily, echoing against the old plaster walls.

"Yeah, you've got to keep a close eye on them," Deb, our team therapist, cautioned as she reached for the basket of chips in the center of the table. "Hey, pass the dip!" The bowl scraped softly across the wood as it made its way down the long table, the air carrying the mingled scents of roasted chicken, garlic, and fried tortillas.

"What do you mean?" Cindy asked, snagging a handful of chips as the basket passed.

"A lot of those kids have been abused," Karen said gently, her tone dropping to match the weight of her words. "They carry anger with nowhere to put it. Sometimes their play becomes more than play—this is the only place they feel safe enough to let it out." Her words seemed to still the room for a beat.

"Man, do we see that in self-defense class! Right, Diane?" Meg chimed in from the far end, pausing to drink deeply from her glass of ice water, the condensation dripping onto the table.

"Yes! Now I understand why they're so eager to learn how to protect themselves," Diane agreed, sliding a platter of roasted chicken and vegetables across the table. "I'm so glad we get to help them, Meg—thanks to you."

"A toast to Meg!" someone called, and we lifted our glasses with weary smiles. The gentle clink of glass against glass carried a note of gratitude, soft laughter loosening the weight of the day. For a moment, the heaviness we all carried was lighter.

"Well, friends, tomorrow morning's going to come fast. Let's eat!" I said, passing a heaping platter of pasta. The sound of forks and plates quickly filled the silence, but in the back of my mind, I knew this day still wasn't quite finished.

Before turning in, we prepared for the next day by counting, sorting, and bagging all the supplies we needed for the following day. On each trip, we selected one of our guest rooms to serve as the holding room for several large boxes of supplies. After dinner, we went to that room and fluffed up, shook out, and refolded the craft of the day, making up for the hours the carefully prepared craft materials spent crammed in boxes as they traveled across the world. We made sure to double-check that we had enough for each child, sometimes counting and recounting. Often, the kids begged us for one or two extra crafts for their siblings who couldn't be at playtime that day.

Serving nearly a hundred children was a monumental task, but somehow, we always had enough stuff and stamina.

I think this is what love looks like in action.

ELENA'S STORY PART THREE
(A fictional tale based on reality)

CONTENT WARNING:

This chapter contains depictions of child trafficking, including familial betrayal and exploitation. Reader discretion is advised.

AND NOW, IMAGINE THIS...

And suddenly, everything changed.

After two years of captivity and unspeakable horror, Elena's world shifted—quietly, unexpectedly—in a single moment.

It began with a knock, soft, measured, and unfamiliar.

The man who entered didn't leer. He didn't bargain.

She was wary—she was always wary—but something in his voice, low and steady, made her pause.

He asked questions—kind ones. He didn't flinch when she looked him in the eye.

He didn't touch her.

He sat on the edge of the cot, not close, and just listened.

Then, just as quietly, he left.

That was strange.

Who was that man?
Why was he asking me those questions?

Elena was confused—but strangely, felt grateful.

Hours later, the walls of her tiny room shook with a deafening crash.

The front door was kicked open.

Boots.

Shouting.

"Stop where you are! Hands behind your back!" a man's voice commanded.

Girls screaming.

"Don't be afraid. You're safe!" another man called out.

Doors slamming open, one after the next.

Elena bolted upright, dazed, heart pounding. She wrapped herself in her threadbare blanket and curled into the corner of the cot, hands shielding her head.

Oh, please, not another raid. Not another punishment.

But this time it was different.

"Give me the keys to this door. Now!" a man called out in a firm voice.

Key in the lock. The door handle turned slowly.

Elena shook violently, unable to move. She squeezed her eyes shut.

A man knelt beside her. Not the one from before.

"Elena," he said softly, "you're safe now."

Safe.

She didn't understand the word. It had long since lost meaning.

Safe.

He coaxed her out, gently, patiently.

Safe.

The light was blinding.

The men wore uniforms, but not like the others. These were real officers.

And then she saw them—her captors—lined up in the street. Hands cuffed behind their backs.

Fresh air brushed her cheeks.

Blue sky arched overhead.

And for the first time in years, Elena felt something stir.

Something she'd nearly forgotten.

Hope.

Is it over? Am I free?

At fourteen, Elena had forgotten how to dream. But now, for the first time in years, she remembered.

The car ride was quiet. Elena sat stiffly in the back seat; her hands tucked beneath her legs. No one pressured her to speak. The woman in the front seat—kind eyes, soft voice—offered a granola bar and a bottle of water. Elena took the water but left the food untouched. She didn't know where they were going and hadn't yet decided what was safe.

When they arrived at the safe house, the gates opened slowly, revealing a white stucco building surrounded by flowering plants and low trees. It wasn't fancy. It didn't need to be. The air smelled fresh and clean. A woman swept the front step. Somewhere nearby, she heard girls laughing.

Inside, she was met by another woman whose smile (warm and not forced) helped calm her. She led her to her room. As they walked down a hallway, the woman said, "You are completely safe. You are okay. Rest now."

Her room, though simple, smelled faintly of lavender. A soft blanket surrounded her bed, and a small, colorful pillow looked handmade. On the windowsill, a blue ceramic mug filled with colored pencils sat on top of a stack of white paper.

There were no locks on the inside of the door. *There's a window!*

Elena peeked out. It overlooked a courtyard with brightly colored flowers and tall trees with large, broad leaves. Several girls sat in a circle on long, stone benches, talking and laughing.

A pair of pajamas was laid out for her at the end of her bed. They were pale yellow with white flowers and soft to the touch. She held them tightly to her chest as she continued to walk around her room.

Later, the same woman who brought her to her room delivered a bowl of soup and bread, and, smiling, left without insisting that she eat. Elena sat on the edge of the bed for a long time before tasting the soup. Finally, she sipped a spoonful. It was the best soup she ever tasted. She dipped her bread into the rich broth and took a big bite.

That night, she didn't cry. She didn't sleep, either. She remained curled on top of the blanket. But for the first time in a long while, no one came for her.

The silence wasn't threatening.

It was just silence.

It was safe.

And in that stillness, with the faint hum of a fan in the corner and the soft scent of lavender in the air, Elena began to realize that maybe—just maybe—she was somewhere she could begin again.

Elena watched as the morning sun lit up the sky. The long hours of not being afraid gave her the kind of rest she hadn't known she needed. She lay quietly and watched the slow movement of shadows as the sun rose.

A gentle knock at the door startled her. A woman peeked in, smiling, holding a bundle of clothes. "Good morning, Elena. We will have breakfast soon. You're welcome to join us when you're ready."

The clothes were soft and clean. She didn't recognize the girl in the mirror, not yet, but something about her didn't look trapped anymore. Elena changed slowly, noticing for the first time how thin her arms had become. She hadn't realized how long her hair was now, almost reaching her waist.

Outside her room, a hallway opened into a spacious area filled with morning light. Through one doorway, she saw shelves of books and art supplies. Through another, a group of girls, maybe six or seven of them, gathered around a table and ate. A few giggled softly. They all wore outfits similar to hers: cotton pants and a short-sleeved T-shirt in a variety of cheerful colors.

They looked normal. Unbelievably normal. *How can this be?*

She stood frozen for a moment until one of the girls looked up. "Hey," the girl said with a friendly smile. "You new?"

Elena nodded.

"You can sit here," the girl said, scooting over and patting the bench beside her. "The toast's good. And they have orange juice today."

Elena hesitated, then slowly walked over, still not quite sure of her surroundings. She sat, barely breathing. Another girl offered her a glass of juice. Someone passed a plate with buttered toast in her direction.

And then, just as she was about to take a bite, a gasp broke the silence.

"Elena?"

She turned to see where the voice came from.

The girl who spoke was smaller than she remembered, with a ragged scar on her eyebrow and the same crooked tooth she had as a child.

"Is it really you?" the girl whispered, and her eyes filled with tears.

"Oh, Lani! I can't believe it!" Elena covered her mouth with her hands, and tears flowed freely as they stepped closer to each other.

It was Lani. They were once best friends, sharing dreams of attending school together. It seemed so long ago now.

They stared at each other as the reality of where they were and why they were there settled in.

And then Elena did something she hadn't done in years.

She smiled.

Later that day, they sat in the garden, knees touching, and traded memories in whispers—what they missed, what they hoped, what they feared. They didn't talk about what happened—not yet. They didn't need to.

A staff member passed by and waved. Elena looked up. The woman wasn't just smiling—she watched Elena like she saw something in Elena that even Elena couldn't see yet.

Surviving is one thing. Healing is another.

That day, she was introduced to the routine: mealtimes shared at long tables under ceiling fans that spun lazily; a morning circle where the girls sang a welcome song—some loudly, some barely mouthing the words; quiet time in the afternoon when books, naps, or drawing were encouraged.

No one asked about her past. It was a common thing to give the girls as much space as possible to acclimate.

Instead, they offered moments—a favorite book, a hand to hold. A joke whispered at lunch made her giggle unexpectedly.

Later in the week, she met a counselor. She didn't sit behind a desk. Instead, she sat cross-legged on a rug scattered with crayons and blocks.

"Want to draw today?" the counselor asked.

Elena nodded, sat down next to the counselor, and chose a purple crayon. The counselor handed her a piece of white paper. She began with a flower, then a tree, and then a little girl under the tree.

That's how it began.

The first steps were always quiet. The girls didn't rush into trusting each other, but the center wasn't in a hurry either. They knew the importance of slowness, of not asking too much, too soon, of allowing joy to feel real again.

Medical check-ups were done with care, and school was offered gently when they were ready. Some dove right in; others waited until their bodies felt less like battlegrounds.

Play was everywhere; it echoed in the courtyard, rang through the classrooms, and spilled into the garden. Laughter often preceded the girls' spoken words. In play, the girls practiced being children again—safe, silly, and seen.

There were setbacks, of course, nights when nightmares returned. There were days when grief came out sideways—in silence, tears, and sudden anger. But no one was shamed for it. This was part of the healing process, too.

One evening, Elena fell asleep during story time, curled up against the shoulder of a house mom. Her breathing was slow and even, a faint smile still on her lips.

Moments like that weren't milestones written on charts, but they were celebrated quietly and reverently by those who understood what they meant.

Healing didn't erase the past. It gave the girls language for what was once unspeakable. It gave them laughter. And over time, it gave them back themselves.

CHAPTER 5
HEALING THROUGH PLAY

"We played pat-a-cake.
I laughed so hard, I forgot to be scared."
Survivor of sex trafficking

PAT-A-CAKE WINS THE DAY

After a particularly sticky afternoon, entertaining 100-plus kids on the third floor of the safe house, my sense of charity waned. Several floor fans valiantly circulated the smelly, thick air around the room, but I thought I might melt away, just like the witch in the Wizard of Oz. The only thing remaining would be two filthy flip-flops on top of what used to be me. By the stoic looks on our team's faces, they felt about the same.

An idea sparked! After conferring with our team leaders, a plan was developed. *Brilliant!* I made my way downstairs to the first floor and sheepishly opened the office door to ask the director for a word. He sat at his desk, several books open in front of him, writing.

"Would it be all right if we split the kids, boys outside and girls stay upstairs, for a couple of hours?"

"Sure!" he looked up from his work, brown eyes twinkling. "Other teams do that all the time."

Deep cleansing breath. *Didn't know that! Oh well, learn as you go, right?*

A few minutes later, through a cloud of dust, fifty boys raced down the stairs and out to the back yard. The boys kicked around several soccer balls in all directions. Dust flew into the air as their feet struck the balls, creating small clouds that mixed with the dry grass, litter, and weeds. The yard, a testament to years of being untended, felt both rugged and wild, and so did their play.

Meanwhile, a woman glanced up briefly and ignored us all as she continued to stoke the outdoor wood fire, where lunch preparations were underway. Upstairs, the girls settled into a craft, all sitting on the floor in a most blissful peace, concentrating on their art projects. *Yahoo!*

About twenty minutes in, I saw two boys fighting in a corner of the yard. The taller boy pushed the other, who struggled to defend himself. Unable to speak the language and not wanting to embarrass them, I stepped between them, and they stopped, looking up at me, a bit surprised. I gave the taller boy a stern look, held his hands up, palms facing out towards me, and started playing pat-a-cake until his frown relaxed and he smiled.

He struggled to follow my lead, so I counted aloud while patting his hands:

"One—two—three—four!" And then, three pats with both hands: "One—two—three!"

The little guy, who moments before had defended himself, laughed and pushed forward, eager for his turn. We played pat-a-cake, laughing together. We learned quickly that these kids don't "pat"; they "smack"—a detail well-known to anyone on the team. Soon, a couple of dozen boys lined up for their turn, leaving my hands red and stinging.

This simple game provided a safe outlet for pent-up aggression and energy. Pat-a-cake! Who knew?

***

TRANSFORMATIVE POWERS OF PLAY

One of the most surprising and beautiful things I witnessed was the profound healing that occurred through pure, simple joy. It wasn't formal therapy or anything official—it was kids laughing, running, being silly, and making up games. It was all the small moments when play took over and worry dropped away, even if just for a little while.

When we played together, you *saw* the change happening. Their faces lit up. Their bodies relaxed. The heaviness lifted. It was as if their hearts remembered something important: that they were still kids, capable of happiness, still whole within.

I realized play wasn't just a distraction—it was a form of medicine. Real medicine.

When the kids drew goofy pictures, raced each other, wrestled with the adult volunteers, or made up songs at the top of their lungs, something deeper happened, too:

- They let go of some of the fear and stress stored inside them.

- They remembered what it felt like to trust, even a little.

- They reconnected to their natural creativity and silliness — the parts untouched by trauma.

- And they built new memories of being safe, free, and loved.

Sometimes the most healing moments were the messiest, noisiest, most ridiculous ones.

Joy made space for healing—real, lasting healing—in ways I never could've planned or foreseen.

I honestly think play is one of the purest forms of hope we have.

OLD MCDONALD'S FARM – A SKIT FOR EVERYONE

Each day, the team presented a skit for the kids. This is one of my favorites. I'm sharing it to give you a taste. It's adaptable for kids everywhere and conveys a powerful message: God loves us all!

Disclaimer: This is not Shakespeare, folks! Simple is better.

The best part about the skits was that the narrator did all the talking, reading from the script. Teammates got to wear funny costumes and ham it up all they wanted. No memorization of lines! This style worked particularly well if any scheduling issues came up. For example, one day, the appointed narrator was asked to help with a house repair job nearby. Another teammate picked up the narrator role with ease.

Remember, the lines had to be interpreted, so everything was repeated. Double the fun! I also think having one narrator speaking made it easier for the kids to grasp, and easier for the one interpreting.

In the script that follows, the narrator's lines are listed one by one, allowing for a pause while the interpreter translates each line.

Honestly, though, as I sit and recall these moments, I would guess that what made the skits so much fun was not the clever words, but a bunch of crazy adults, with goofy, handmade costumes on, hamming it up as much as possible. And what's better than making over-the-top animal sounds!

Old McDonald's Farm by Susan Ernst	Notes / Props
Characters: Farmer McDonald (This character only enters at the end to call his animals.) Cow: A bossy type – self-important Horse: A big shot – thinks he runs the farm Pig: A loud, boisterous type Duck: A timid little guy; he shakes his head all the time and quacks a lot.	Farm Scene: Snacks are scattered on stage for Pig to find. River scene for Rainbow Fish
Act 1 – Scene 1	Animals can be heard arguing, **making a lot of noise** (use animal sounds).
Narrator: McDonald's farm was a beautiful place. It was so peaceful and happy. Wait a minute! This does not sound peaceful and happy! Shhhh! Shhhh! There is so much noise and arguing!	The narrator hushes the animals.
Narrator continues: One morning, all the animals were arguing about who was the most important helper for Farmer McDonald. They each thought that if they were the most helpful, or the strongest, or the smartest, Farmer McDonald would love them the best.	Cow, horse, and pig strut around making animal sounds. The cow takes center stage.

Old McDonald's Farm by Susan Ernst	Notes / Props
Narrator: The cow said, "I'm definitely the most important, because I make milk for Farmer McDonald and his wife."	Cow "moos" loudly for the audience and struts her stuff around the farmyard.
Meanwhile…	Duck keeps shaking his head and stays in the corner of the stage.
Narrator: The horse said, "No, I'm the most important, because I pull the wagon for Farmer McDonald. I am the strongest, too!"	Horse neighs loudly at all the kids to try to scare everyone.
Narrator: The Pig said, "You are both wrong! I am the most important. I eat all the garbage for Farmer McDonald, so there is no mess!"	Pig snorts A LOT and sniffs the ground looking for snacks to eat.
Meanwhile…	All animals leave the stage except for Duck.

Old McDonald's Farm by Susan Ernst	Notes / Props
Act 1 - Scene 2	
Narrator: Well, poor Duck just put his head down and shook it. He did not know what to do. He didn't make milk. He couldn't pull a wagon, and he didn't like eating garbage. He was sure that Farmer McDonald didn't like him. What should he do? Then, he remembered Rainbow Fish! (Note: Rainbow Fish is a colorful, magical, talking fish that was introduced to the kids on day 1. He shows up in a lot of the skits. He is very wise!)	Duck waddles back and forth, covering his face with his wings, quacking softly.
Narrator continues: Rainbow Fish is so wise! He will know just what to do.	So, Duck starts down the road, waddling as fast as he can go! And Quacking!

Old McDonald's Farm by Susan Ernst	Notes / Props
Act 2 – Scene 1	
Narrator: Duck went down to the river and waded in. He stuck his head in the water looking for Rainbow Fish. He came back up and, shaking the water off his head, he said: "I can't see Rainbow Fish."	Duck puts his head down behind the river prop and comes back up as if he had been underwater.
Narrator continues: "I think we ALL need to call Rainbow Fish so he can hear us. Will you call him with me? Kids join Duck: "Rainbow fish, are you there? Rainbow fish, we need you!"	The other farm animals appear, standing quietly off to the side. Rainbow Fish appears.
Narrator: (Rainbow Fish) "Well, well, well, what can I do for you?" Narrator speaks: (Duck) "We are arguing about who Farmer McDonald loves the best. I don't think I do as much as they do. So, how could Farmer McDonald love me? He might even eat me for dinner!"	Rainbow Fish pokes up behind the river scene. Duck hangs his head. Waddles in circles. Quacks softly, flapping wings.

Old McDonald's Farm by Susan Ernst	Notes / Props
Narrator: (Rainbow Fish) It looks like you all have forgotten something very important. Farmer McDonald loves all his animals, just like God loves all his children. It does not matter how strong you are, like Horse. Or if you can make milk, like Cow. Or if you can clean up all the scraps, like Pig. Or, if you are just kind and happy, like you, Duck. The Farmer loves you all the same. His love is a gift to all of you. You don't have to do or be anything special to get it. His love is always there for you.	
Narrator: Rainbow Fish dove down into the water and swam away. Narrator: The horse said, "He loves us all the same. No one deserves more love than the other. How wonderful for us!"	The animals are all quiet. The horse shakes his head and neighs, prancing around the stage.

Old McDonald's Farm by Susan Ernst	Notes / Props
Narrator: Just then, the animals could hear Farmer McDonald calling. Here, Cow! Here, Horse! Here, Pig! Here, my little Duck! Please come home! I love you all, and it's time for dinner!	Farmer McDonald appears on stage, in the corner, holding his hand up to his mouth to call for animals.
Narrator: Of course, the pig ran faster than anyone! The End! It's time to sing the Old McDonald song we learned yesterday and wear the hats you made today!	Teammates help kids put on their hats, and teens start the song!

The kids loved to sing *Old McDonald Had a Farm!* If we were willing, they would've sung that song every day! They loved making animal noises and acting out, copying our distinguished actors!

CHAPTER 6
LOVE AS A FORCE OF TRANSFORMATION

> "They didn't try to fix me.
> They just loved me until I could start to heal."
> Survivor of sex trafficking

A SOFT PILLOW TO REST MY HEAD

I mentioned earlier that when it came to building the team that served at this rescue center, sacred work was at hand. I've never seen such a perfect mix of talents and personalities, all linked by one common thread: to serve those kids the best way we knew how.

We were fortunate to have a very talented craft designer. She dedicated months to her research, planning, and developing crafts suitable for this mission. We were told to plan for about 125 kids (knowing that this would be plenty and most likely provide extras, which always found a home). Consideration was given to the age range of the kids we'd serve, from very small to teens. The crafts had to withstand the journey from America to somewhere across the globe. They couldn't be too heavy. They shouldn't be too expensive. Ideally, they shouldn't require too many supplies or tools to bring them to life. They couldn't be too difficult, considering the language barrier and the range of ages, and we had to keep time in mind, as the days were filled with many different activities for the children.

On this day, the craft was a pillow made from soft, colorful fleece. Each pillow consisted of two pieces of fleece cut in the shape of a large square. Cuts were made along the edge of each side, about three inches in depth, creating a fringe. By placing the sides together and matching up the fringes on each side, the kids tied two corresponding fringe pieces together in a simple knot. The kids worked around each of the four sides of their pillows until a small opening remained. They stuffed their pillows with filling material (polyester fiberfill). Once filled, they tied the remaining fringes. Easy? Only if you know how to tie a knot!

This was, by far, one of the most popular crafts. Having seen where many of these children lived and how they lived, one could easily understand why. This was a precious treasure! The craft was easy for the older kids to teach the little ones, making for a happy day for all concerned!

We sat on the wooden floor of the huge playroom. Each team member found their spot, and the teens counted the number of kids, sending an equal number of kids to each team member. So, about ten kids per adult, all sitting in a circle. The crafter, with some help from other teammates, handed out the supplies to each circle. Once we were all ready, our crafter stood at the head of the room and demonstrated how to make the pillow.

Once we began our work, the challenges we faced surfaced quickly. The little guys couldn't tie the knots. So, as all good teams do, we punted. We ensured that each circle had a good mix of older kids and younger kids. Where needed, we rearranged the kids. The team members and older kids helped the little ones tie their knots. The kids, all ages, were enthralled. They watched intently as an adult, either a woman or a man, tied the knots. When the adult encouraged the little one to try, they did, as best they could, and if they needed help, they got it. The stuffing part was easy and fun. It was pure joy to see that we settled on a craft that both the young kids and the teens loved. As the pillows were completed, the magic started. I won't forget this for a long time.

I sat with my group, finishing up pillows for the youngest of the kids. The older kids began their play, and the younger ones were anxious to join them. I looked around the room and saw that my teammates were all at about the same stage. Some of our older kids grabbed their pillows and, moving away from the little kids, found a place to lie down on the floor and rest their heads on their new cushy pillows. Some of the kids, no surprise, started batting each other with their pillows, and if the laughter continued, we tolerated their fun new game. Some of the small kids clutched their pillows to their chests, holding onto them for dear life.

Meanwhile, our crafter sat with her circle of kids. She was pooped, and rightly so. I watched as several of her new soulmates approached her, sitting cross-legged on the floor, to show her their pillow. Each time, she covered her mouth with her hands, as if surprised, and exclaimed, "Oh! How beautiful!" And the child beamed even brighter.

In a moment of sweet tenderness, this special teammate sat on the floor, knees drawn to her chest. She rested her head on her folded arms, which rested on her knees. With a gentle pat on her shoulder and pointing at the little girl's pillow, she invited her to take a rest. Smiling with understanding, the little girl placed her pillow on my teammate's back and, with innocent trust, rested her head on the pillow and closed her eyes. They remained in this heartwarming position for several minutes.

LISTENING WITHOUT FIXING

"Mom, I know you. You're going to try to fix each kid, and you won't be able to."

Wow. Thanks for the vote of confidence, I thought, knowing my daughter was probably right.

"What you can do is love them. Do that! That is a good thing, and it will help them to heal." Wise words from my daughter as I prepared for the trip.

As I mentioned earlier, our job was laid out for us very clearly: "Love those kids. Give them a reason to hope."

It's not the job of the teams that come for a week or two to "fix it." The facility has full-time counselors and social workers who are the "fixers."

That said, our team included a couple of psychotherapists, as well as Karen Marks, co-leader, who has a master's in psychology. This team dedicated a portion of their time to the full-time counselors, social workers, and house moms at the live-in centers for the rescued girls. They provided specialized group therapy sessions, providing some relief for counselors suffering from vicarious trauma; that is, trauma caused by listening to dozens of traumatic stories every day. The therapists provided a safe environment for the counselors and social workers to share their feelings and work on tools that dispelled their anxiety and stress, and continue to counsel the rescued girls.

Although it's never been our job as volunteers to fix the problems these children carry, one of the most important things we can do is listen—really listen—with our whole heart. The children at the center often crave connection and attention, and it's not unusual for a child to form a bond with a volunteer. They may come to know us, trust us, even love us—and when that happens, they may begin to share their story.

That's when we must remind ourselves: we're here to listen, not solve. Our presence, our open hearts, our willingness to hold space for their words without jumping in with solutions—that's the gift. Research backs this up, of course, showing that being truly heard helps people regulate their emotions and build resilience. You can see it on a child's face when they realize you're not going anywhere—that you're simply there with them in that moment.

Listening is one of the purest acts of love we can offer. It means showing up fully, without distraction, and letting that child know: "I see you. I hear you. Your story matters." In a place where trust has so often been broken, this kind of presence helps rebuild it.

Of course, the center's trained staff handles the deeper therapeutic work. They're experts in radical listening and trained to intervene when needed. As volunteers, we must respect that and know our role. In short, we stay in our lane. But that doesn't mean our listening doesn't matter. Every moment we spend being present with a child without trying to fix, rescue, or explain contributes to healing.

The center is meant to be a place where kids feel safe enough to speak, cry, laugh, or sit in silence if that's what they need. No judgment. No pressure. Just love. That kind of space doesn't just happen; it's created through empathy, time, and trust.

Listening without fixing is one of the quiet superpowers of this work. And even though it might feel small, it's not. It's huge. Because in those tender moments of being heard, healing begins.

A WORD ABOUT RESILIENCE

The more time I spent with the kids, the more I realized that joy and play weren't just moments of escape—they were signs of something much bigger at work inside them.

What we witnessed we called resilience—powerful, breathtaking resilience.

Many of these kids experienced things no child should ever have to face. Abuse, abandonment, poverty, hunger, fear—it was all part of their story. And yet somehow, their spirits weren't broken. Their hearts still leaned toward hope. They still laughed. They still dreamed. They still reached for connection. Was this resilience, or something else?

I think great care is needed when speaking of resilience. There are mixed views on this word. Here's mine.

The definition of resilience:

Able to withstand or recover quickly from difficult conditions.

Synonyms:

Pliability, flexibility, suppleness, plasticity, springiness.

Makes one wonder, are we talking about a tree in the wind, or a human being?

Most of the kids joined us each day, appearing gleeful and ready to play! The fact that the kids hadn't lost their access to their joy or capacity for play was surprising. Initially, we labeled this *resilience*.

In discussing this with a psychotherapist, I discovered that the children's responses were "probably more likely activated by a mixture of feelings, some having to do with genuine relief and the playful capacity of children. Others may have been a trauma response coming from their particular adaptations, especially in this case, to the common 'fawn response' adapted early on to appease an abuser and stay safe."

When evaluating the children's resilience, we must consider the dire situations that led them to daycare and the safe house. **We must acknowledge that until those 'dire situations' (child abuse and child sex trafficking) are abolished, we must take great care in evaluating what we're labeling as resilience, when it could simply be a mask that works, until it doesn't.**

One problem with traumatized children is that when they transition to a safe environment, their survival responses don't turn off.

Clinical Psychologist Dr. Patricia Crittenden shows us that all children are very instinctive and wise at organizing their behavior around danger. Crittenden teaches that: Attachment is not the problem; danger is the problem, and attachment is the solution.

Here is an excerpt from Dr. Crittenden's work:

"Traumatized children tend to develop one main attachment strategy, which could be either Insecure Avoidant or Insecure Preoccupied.

Avoidant children learn early on that showing their feelings and having needs brings on danger or makes their parent/caregiver withdraw. They learn the mantra, 'To keep safe and to keep others close, I must hide my emotions and look as if everything is okay.' Inside, they feel frightened, vulnerable, worthless, grieving, and hopeless, but on the outside, they often seem bright, fine, competent, and often even 'the clown of the class.' These children are often not a concern to parents/caregivers and teachers until later childhood because they do not show 'behavioral problems,' until they are triggered by something stressful or a developmental milestone, and then they emotionally 'fall apart.'"

Dr. Crittenden defines the Insecure Preoccupied child:

"These children learn early on that showing feelings and 'big behaviors' is the only way to get noticed and keep parents/caregivers nearby. They learn the mantra, 'To keep safe and others close by, I must exaggerate my behavior and emotions, and I must be angry/upset for as long as possible, because if I lose my parent/caregiver, I don't know when I will get them back again.' Inside, these children feel petrified, anxious, worthless, and unlovable; on the outside, they appear rageful, aggressive, hostile, disruptive, and rude. These children bounce from one irresolvable crisis to the next. To have an adult solve the crisis would be too frightening, as it means the adult may disappear. Children who use this strategy are often successful at disarming the adult's angry response by becoming vulnerable or needy."[1]

Based on my observations, I'd say we were witnessing "Insecure Avoidant Attachment" as well as trauma response. Given what we learned about these children's daily lives and the prolific child abuse and/or trafficking in their area, this makes the most sense.

In Lys Eden's (social work student) post, *The Problem with Resilience,* she says, "Whilst describing a child as 'resilient' can appear empowering, equally, it can perpetuate superhero rhetoric in which some children are perceived as having some inherent superhuman strength to withstand adversity. The messages that children may internalize from this are ones fraught with perfectionism and self-sustenance. They may learn that they only receive praise when they appear strong and able to cope (with pressures that no child should ever have to cope with, I hasten to add) and may keep things to themselves in order to appease those around them. This may reinforce the pre-existing coping strategy and prevent the underlying feelings of shame, inadequacy, and desperate need for intimacy from being shown and acknowledged."[2]

---

1. https://beaconhouse.org.uk/wp-content/uploads/2020/02/Developmen-tal-Trauma-Close-Up-Revised-Jan-2020.pdf

2. https://richarddevinesocialwork.com/2020/08/14-the-problem-with-resilience/

There is much more to learn on this subject, but for now, I want to emphasize care when we use the word 'resilience' when describing a traumatized child. Resilience is multifaceted, perhaps ranging from moments of great strength to moments of vulnerability.

I think we should acknowledge that the rescue facility provides a consistently safe place for the kids attending daycare to have capacity for play, albeit temporarily. The underlying risk of exploitation is real. No child, resilient or not, should be faced with this dilemma. Our attention must be focused in significant part on fighting child abuse and sex trafficking, and at the same time, supporting the rescue facilities around the globe that provide a haven for the vulnerable.

CHAPTER 7
WRITINGS FROM VOLUNTEER TEAM MEMBERS (2015-2019)

"I used to think the world didn't see me. Then someone showed up, week after week, just to play. That's when I started to believe I was worth showing up for."

Survivor of Sex Trafficking

In the pages that follow, you'll hear directly from some of my teammates. I invited each of them to share a meaningful takeaway from their time serving, but what they offered was so much more.

As each story arrived in my inbox, my heart swelled with memories and a deep sense of gratitude. I'm proud of all we gave, but more than that, I'm humbled by the extraordinary privilege of being part of it.

This was love, transformed into action. And together, these stories reveal the true heart of our mission.

BY DIANE BLALOCK, TEAM CO-LEADER

On each mission trip, we poured love on the young teens rescued from trafficking or living in extreme poverty who found a life and purpose in the loving arms of this ministry. Susan Ernst, a born teacher and loving spirit, wanted to teach an English class that would help these kids in their conversations with volunteers from the States. On our last day, Susan gathered the teens around our table.

"What are your dreams for the future?" Susan asked. They come from crushing poverty and unspeakable abuse. But they receive love, support, therapy, and an education through the ministry where we volunteered. They gave back, too. They help with the younger kids. They contribute to all aspects of this ministry while continuing to dream and work toward their future.

On that morning, in the growing heat of the day, sitting on resin chairs, we looked into each other's eyes. "Tell me what you want to be when you grow up?" Susan asked each teen sitting in that circle.

Every one of them had a dream. They wanted to be teachers, nurses, actors, singers, managers, and own their own businesses. Every one of them had a different dream. I looked at Susan and saw the love she had for them, and I watched her give them strength and hope. Taking the hand of each teen after they spoke, Susan said, "God bless you. Your dream is very possible. We will keep you in prayer." They listened to each other in silent wonder as their friends spoke from their hearts. Many expressed surprise and enthusiasm for the other's dreams.

It was a soaring experience that still brings a lump to my throat and tears to my eyes. Susan found a way to reach each student and give them her love. I'll never forget the honor of being in that moment with Susan and those teens. We all have dreams. But how many times do we ask someone what those dreams are? And then, listen with our whole heart and soul? It's life-changing.

ABOUT THE SELF-DEFENSE CLASS

One of our teammates, Meg, is an expert in martial arts and developed a class for the older teens and young adults in self-defense. I served alongside her. I couldn't help but think, *How will the young men react to learning self-defense from a woman, given their country's culture?* I thought they'd be polite and nothing more. I couldn't have been more mistaken. They were deeply interested in what Meg taught and asked many questions. In my naivety, I thought men were safe in this culture and women were the victims. Wrong again. The young men suffered beatings at school for being Christians. They were jumped and robbed as they walked through their village. They were desperate to learn ways to protect themselves in their violent world.

The young women were very attentive and quickly absorbed all Meg taught.   Toward the end of the week, they felt comfortable enough to ask the questions weighing on their hearts.

"How can we defend ourselves when more than one man attacks us?" one woman asked. A chill ran down my spine as she calmly asked her question. I looked at her classmates, and they calmly looked at Meg for the answer to her question. With horror, I remembered how gang rape was a huge issue for not only young girls, but all the women in this country, and this was at the heart of her seemingly simple question.

Meg said later that day, "I've never been asked that question in the States. The shocking savagery of their everyday lives was overwhelming to me." She quickly worked up a lesson plan for fending off multiple attackers and rapists.

We saw that it didn't matter what their gender or age was. They live in a violent world that's light-years from ours. Their everyday reality is one of trying to survive not only from crushing poverty but also from incredible violence. And my fervent prayer is that what they learned helps keep them safe.

DIANE BLALOCK

Diane was a news wire reporter and worked for ABC radio stations in San Francisco. She is a commercial real estate appraiser specializing in the hospitality industry. Diane was a co-leader for international teams fighting sex trafficking. Diane is active at the Presbyterian Church of Novato and is the director of video services. She also serves on the community life and outreach team.

BY KAREN MARKS, TEAM CO-LEADER

"Do the rescued girls hit you?" Our team's therapist asked the counselors at the live-in rescue center.

The counselors all answered "Yes."

Our therapist nodded and asked, "And how do you feel when you're being hit?"

They all had the same answer: "Angry! Why are you doing this to me?"

Our therapist then said, "Yes, you are feeling what those girls feel when they're being assaulted: *You're hurting me! I don't deserve this!*"

As the training continued, our therapist asked whether they had ever had recurring nightmares from the stories they heard. "Yes," they all said. One offered, "I wake up pushing away my phantom attacker and trying to scream." They all nodded and shared similar stories of their vicarious trauma.

It's impossible not to feel the full range of emotions—overwhelming anger toward the men who inflict this incomprehensible horror, sadness for the lifetime of recovery ahead for these sweet girls, and compassion and awe at the women (and men) who devote their lives to stopping this torture and providing care for the rescued girls. The comments from the counselors confirmed that the ripple effects of that abuse travel outward in all directions—to loved ones, caregivers, and the larger community.

An hour later, we joined the center's staff in the warm, humid lunchroom. I was overwhelmed to be in the presence of so many rescued girls. There were perhaps 60 girls, ranging in age from maybe 7 to 15, all sitting at the long picnic-style tables we all remember from our childhood lunchrooms. They appeared so typical. Some teased each other, laughed, or talked quietly with each other. Some seemed lively, others shy.

I said a silent prayer: *From now on, may they all be safe and feel loved.* And then, as I looked at the faces of the staff, I realized: *These adults are doing just that!* They rescued, counseled, taught, and lived with the girls, giving them safety, love, and kindness. My prayer was being answered. I remain in awe of these women changing this world, one little girl at a time.

KAREN MARKS

Karen lives in Novato, California. She co-led the teams that traveled internationally to support the organization that rescues and rehabilitates girls who are victims of child sex trafficking. Karen earned her M.S. in Organizational Psychology/Change Management and worked at various companies in that field. She is currently working with a team to provide training to reduce suicide.

BY JOHN MARKS

One of my most cherished memories of our service at the community outreach center was when the at-risk children arrived for their bible school activities. The staff at the center drove vans out to the poorest neighborhoods where the factories were located to pick up children and bring them back to the center. One day, when the van doors opened, the kids jumped for joy, leaping out of the vans and screaming as they ran full speed into the building. They scampered up the stairs to the large room, where they spent the next few hours singing, playing games, making crafts, watching Bible story skits, and, most of all, receiving unconditional love and support from the young staff and volunteer teams in a safe environment. They looked forward to this experience! It was as if they had arrived at the front entrance to Disneyland!

Some of the kids we served came from the houses along the river nearby. I worked with a team that made repairs to those houses. The houses were all constructed on stilts due to the rising river levels during the rainy season. During the drier season, the houses had many wooden steps leading into the main house entry. During the rainy season, the river rose to just below the main floor, so no steps were necessary.

I'll never forget the children who lived there. Several of them wore necklaces they made at the daycare center in the rescue facility. They recognized us and proudly showed their crafts to us as we walked by—one of my favorite memories.

JOHN MARKS

John resides in Novato, California, and is a retired human resources executive and consultant. Following retirement, he served for two years as a volunteer grant writer for a Christian NGO whose mission was to end child sex trafficking. He participated in five overseas church mission trips to serve an NGO dedicated to the fight against child sex trafficking. His service included teaching basic computer skills, assisting in home construction, and participating in children's bible school activities at community outreach centers.

BY JORDAN MARKS

I worked and traveled in Australia in 2017 and planned a three-month backpacking trip through Southeast Asia. My mom suggested I join her, my dad, my aunt, and their entire team from their church to help out on their mission trip. They served at an organization in that region that rescues girls from trafficking.

"You only need to stay a few days," my mom said, "but you can stay longer if that works out for you." I knew ahead of time that there would be something incredibly special about this trip and the community we served.

Although we did some sightseeing in the area, most of our time was spent at the organization's facilities. I remember how bright these kids were! I was told I would help teach kids computer skills and navigate the web, but upon arrival, I found the kids already logged in online, playing a game that taught them English. They were already light-years ahead of the curriculum! One of the reasons why these kids were so far ahead was that the "in-country" teenagers and young adults provided great instruction and leadership for the younger kids.

One memory that stands out was when we performed skits for the children from Bible stories. Our team brought a brown wig and beard for someone to be Jesus. I had long hair and a beard at that time, so I was already well-equipped, in that sense, to play that role. The mission team didn't expect me to stay the whole time, but I was so touched by these children and everyone who worked there. If I had an opportunity to leave the children a little happier in any way, then staying a whole week became a foregone conclusion.

These children and the entire community have been through so much. The whole trip was an incredibly inspiring and life-changing experience.

JORDAN MARKS

Jordan was born and raised in Novato, California. He attended Purdue University in Indiana and has spent time living in Brazil, Australia, and Romania. He is currently a UX Designer living in Des Moines, Iowa, and enjoys traveling, surfing, scuba diving, being with family and friends, and all kinds of animals.

BY ALLISON MARKS

I was a registered pediatric intensive care nurse for a little over a year when I decided to join a team of adults going to serve an organization that rescued and rehabilitated girls who had been trafficked. My role was to work at the free medical clinic, providing care for the locals who suffered and couldn't afford to go to the doctor. The organization we supported was tackling the trafficking issue from all angles, including providing free medical care to the local residents who struggled with illnesses and injuries. This clinic was the only one of its kind and provided hope and care to many people. About 20-25 people, at any one time, waited to be seen by a doctor or nurse. In this country, nurses can diagnose illnesses and prescribe medications.

As I sat in the clinic, I felt intimidated. *I don't know the language. What use can I be? I'm primarily familiar with treating children, not adults.* Yet my interpreter was exceptionally kind and skilled and knew how to translate their issues or symptoms.

One woman waited for quite some time. She held a small child, perhaps a year and a half old, who was very tired and sleepy, appearing quite ill. I listened to her lungs and determined that, among other symptoms, she was severely dehydrated and working hard to breathe. I was concerned enough that I grabbed the doctor right away. "You will need to take your daughter to the local hospital as soon as possible," the doctor advised the mother. We arranged for her to take her daughter to the hospital that morning.

As I think back on that morning, I realized: *I was able to make a difference in the well-being of that little girl and her very worried mother.* All of us, including the interpreter, the doctor, and others on our team, might have saved that little girl's life that day.

ALLISON MARKS

Allison is a registered pediatric ICU nurse, working at the UCSF Children's Hospital in San Francisco. She grew up in Novato, California, graduated from UC Davis and Samuel Merritt College with bachelor's degrees, and currently lives in Petaluma. She loves to travel, ski, hike, camp, and spend time with family, friends, her two dogs, and a cat.

BY MARGIE BETTS

I sat in the airplane and wondered if my decision to come on this journey to serve was the right one. Our group made our devotions, said our prayers asking God to help us in our service, and prepared (no detail too small) down to the extra eyelashes sewn on the puppet. And yet, *am I ready for this?* I had so many questions. *Can anything I do make a real difference in a place so full of poverty and hardship?*

As the plane landed, I prayed as I remembered the words of the Psalm: "Commit your way to the Lord; trust in him and he will do this." *Okay, Lord, I will do this with your help.* I'm an art teacher who loves teaching young children, so with a lot of help from our group, I wrote some puppet plays, acquired a puppet stage, and puppets.

On the first day of our daycare class, I looked out from behind the puppet stage and saw at least 80 or 90 children of all ages, and even babies held by their mothers. I was apprehensive. *Will they understand the stories? Will they like puppets?* So many questions. Yet again, the words "trust in Him" came into my mind. I became my puppet, Pippa, the little girl with outrageous eyelashes who said funny things to the children and did crazy dances across the puppet stage.

By the time our service mission ended, all the children were laughing and screaming her name, begging her to come on the puppet stage and dance with them. How could I have been so apprehensive? There was so much love in that huge room. In those weeks, Pippa's light shone out to all the children, and they reflected it back with love and laughter. It was a priceless gift I'll always be grateful for. Now, when I feel sad or old or life is difficult, I channel my inner Pippa and see the smiles and hear the laughter again and know I need to trust in God and all will be right.

MARGIE BETTS

Disney uses the word "Imagineer" to describe their creative employees. Margie Betts feels that word best describes her. A graduate of Carnegie Mellon University, she has traveled the world for major retailers but found her love teaching art to children in elementary and middle school, and now, in retirement, volunteering to teach in schools without art programs.

BY DEBRA ROESLER

I provided training to the young women on-site who counseled those rescued from life-threatening situations. The survivors were placed in safe houses so they could restart their lives and embrace God. Our work included teaching the house moms at the children's shelter. *How can I support counselors who have experienced cumulative traumas, many of whom are survivors?*

I planned what I could teach based on what was culturally appropriate. I looked forward to the smiles on their faces and the excitement they felt when they received the training. The house moms, wearing mostly PJs, arrived each day, smiling, with their notebooks and pens. I felt like we were all family.

Over the four years I served, I felt sad when we departed, as I re-entered my life, free to be my own person and live a life of my choosing. This became a moral conflict with me as I specialize in working with Post-Traumatic Stress Disorder (PTSD). How can these amazing people smile through the pain of living and rebuilding their lives? At least two-thirds suffered from PTSD, high unemployment, were desperately poor, chronically depressed, and subject to violence. I questioned my ability to make a difference, feeling like an impostor. I was spiritually and emotionally conflicted, and angry at a world that allowed this beautiful country to suffer.

How can I accept beauty, hardship, and trauma at the same time? *Can I hold space for both?* I questioned where my heart was torn. *Am I called to serve or rescue? How can I be gracious when I'm not suffering or living in poverty?* I began to have peace with the idea that you can hold two truths at the same time—bad and good. Anger and love can coexist. You can love God and have faith that with empathy, you can accept what is and do your best. I found peace when I accepted the many conflicting truths that our mission entailed.

DEB ROESLER

Deb is a licensed psychotherapist with over 10 years of experience specializing in trauma and PTSD with first responders and the military. Deb served on active duty for 22 years in the U.S. Army and is now retired, finding a calling to help those struggling with cumulative trauma.

BY ELIZA ROESLER

A lasting memory I'll never forget from my two years volunteering with this team was a moment I shared with the pastor's son. He was about five years old at the time and spoke English impressively. He sat with me each day at lunch, and we found our own way to communicate and chat, mainly by swapping simple phrases in his native language for silly English ones, while using animated hand gestures to fill in the gaps.

From day one, he said the same phrase. We sounded it out together over that week, and by the end of the week, I had learned it. I knew it was a term of endearment and affection, but he finally told me in the last goodbye ceremony what it meant. "I love you." It was the first and last thing he had said to me on that trip.

Feeling God's love through cultural and language barriers was something I hadn't experienced firsthand before, and it's something I'll never forget. When I got home, I got a tattoo of the phrase to remind me of a greater purpose to serve, connect with, and love all of God's children. This continues to guide me as I try to lead with compassion and love in all things, from my career in healthcare to my faith and everyday life.

ELIZA ROESLER

Eliza went on two trips with the team in 2018 and 2019. She turned 18 on the second trip, an unforgettable and special birthday. Eliza worked primarily in the center with the children. She credits this trip as her first calling to international service.

BY CINDY AMADEA

Before we left on our mission trip, our team read *Ministering Cross-Culturally*. One of its core lessons was this: if you want to serve well, you must first seek to understand the people you're serving. Their culture, their challenges, their way of life, it all matters.

Some of the children who came to the shelter each day lived with their families at a nearby factory. One afternoon, our team visited that factory. That's when the reality behind some of their stories truly came into focus for me.

A man stepped out of one of the dilapidated shacks that sat behind the factory—the place he and his family called home. He approached the team, eager to talk.

"The factory is going to be sold soon," he said with a sense of urgency. His voice carried the weight of generational debt, the fear of unemployment, and the uncertainty of being transferred to another, unknown factory.

"I have no idea how we will survive if that happened," he added, his eyes pleading. His family lived in extreme poverty.

"I don't know where our next meal would come from if they sold the factory," he said, his eyes filled with tears.

What he said next made my heart skip a beat. "I'm worried about my children. They love coming to the shelter's daycare. They are safe there while I work. What will happen to them if we lose that?"

In that moment, my perspective shifted. Until then, I had been viewing everything through my lens—my assumptions, my limited understanding. But now I saw the world through his eyes. I could no longer impose my frame of reference on his reality. Mine was too small. I hadn't grasped the weight he carried. But now, I could feel it.

CINDY AMADEA

Cindy resides in Novato, California. She retired from the Golden Gate Bridge, Highway and Transportation District as the Ferry Division Superintendent in 2018 after 32 years of service. She and her husband, Izzat, have been married for 43 years, and are blessed with two sons and one daughter, four grandchildren, and one on the way. Cindy enjoys caring for those grandkids, traveling, reading, and hiking.

BY MEG FIANDACA

I still remember my first mission trip, overwhelmed by the extreme poverty and the scale of trafficking. I thought, *I'm just one person. How can I possibly make a difference?* But with each visit, that belief began to shift. What I've come to understand is that even brief moments of service can create real change. By simply showing up, offering kindness, and sharing our unique gifts, we have the power to touch lives. You never know how much a smile or heartfelt conversation might mean to someone. Sometimes, that small gesture is exactly what they need most.

When I arrived at class with my amazing partner, Diane, we met girls ranging in age from nine years old to about 18. All were victims of horrible abuse, and several were still physically bruised or burned.

We knew that our self-defense class couldn't change their past; it couldn't heal their wounds and wouldn't give them all the tools they needed to protect themselves. But what it could do was allow them to be in an environment of empowerment and love from two American women who traveled across the globe to pour into them.

Every day, we started and ended class by yelling "I am strong!" in their native language and English several times. We played games to make learning self-defense fun. The result? On the last day, I was handed a card from some of the house moms that said, "It has been encouraging to hear them yell, 'I am strong!' every day when we often hear the difficult and broken words that come out of their mouths. Thank you for speaking truth and life into them." As we were leaving one day, one of the nine-year-old girls, who was the most shut down that week, stuck her head out of her bedroom window, smiled, and yelled, "I am strong!" at us.

I doubt any of them remember the moves we taught them, but I do know that a fundamental difference was made in their hearts, which can create lasting change.

MEG FIANDACA

Meg is a 3rd-degree black belt in mixed martial arts and has taught both youth and adults a wide variety of martial arts styles since 2019. She has taught survivors of trafficking and at-risk youth. Meg is an avid mountain trail runner and loves spending time with her teen daughter and husband, both 1st-degree black belts.

WHAT WE LEARNED FROM THE KIDS' COURAGE

Being around these kids, you couldn't help but be changed. Their tenacity wasn't just something we witnessed—it was something that *taught* us, shaped us, and challenged us.

They showed us what real courage looks like. Not the kind you see in movies, loud and flashy—but the quiet, everyday kind. The kind that keeps reaching out for love even after being hurt. The kind that dares to trust again, even with a bruised heart.

The kind that chooses to hope, even when the world has given them every reason not to.

In so many ways, the children became our teachers. Their courage lit a path for us, showing us what it means to live with open hearts, regardless of the circumstances.

If we could, we'd tell you exactly where we went and show you every face that changed our lives. But the truth is, protecting the girls we served means keeping that part of the story off the page.

What we can share is what it felt like to be there—ten of us, strangers at first, learning to serve with open hands and open hearts. The place isn't the point, the people are. And the transformation we experienced—both theirs and ours.

CHAPTER 8

WHAT HAPPENS AFTER RESCUE: A CLOSER LOOK

> "Healing isn't about forgetting. It's about learning to
> live with what happened and still choosing to believe
> in love, in hope, and myself."
>
> Survivor of sex trafficking

THE HEALING JOURNEY

The steps described in the following paragraphs reflect common practices across international safe houses and restoration centers, many of which follow trauma-informed models similar to those advocated by organizations like Hagar International, Love146, and the International Justice Mission.

When a girl is rescued from trafficking and brought to a safe house, what happens next might not look dramatic to an outsider. There's no fanfare, no grand turning point. But make no mistake—what follows is sacred ground. Healing begins, not with words, but with warmth, safety, and human kindness.

A girl steps through the door carrying the invisible weight of all she's survived. Sometimes she's silent. Sometimes guarded, even angry. And sometimes she collapses into the arms of someone who says, "You're safe now." That moment alone is life-changing.

First, it's about the basics: a warm meal, a bath, clean clothes, and a soft bed—a place where no one is going to hurt her, where no one wants anything from her. Those simple things—things most of us take for granted—are acts of deep restoration.

In the days that follow, the staff gently begin to assess what she needs. Not just physically, but emotionally and spiritually. It's never rushed. Trust comes slowly and on her terms. One caregiver may sit beside her day after day, asking nothing, offering a smile or a quiet moment of play. Healing doesn't begin with questions. It starts with presence.

There's a rhythm to life in a safe house. Structure helps the girls feel secure knowing when meals are served, when it's time for school, and when bedtime comes. Routines, once used to control them in trafficking situations, are now used to comfort and stabilize. The girls begin to feel a sense of control over their own days.

Eventually, when she's ready, she's offered counseling. It might be one-on-one therapy with someone trained in trauma care, or it might be through art, music, or dance. Sometimes it starts with crayons and silence. And sometimes, healing begins when another girl says, "Me too."

Over time, she begins to reclaim her childhood through education, life skills, and friendship. Some girls catch up on years of missed schooling. Others learn how to cook, sew, care for a garden, or take on a vocational skill. These aren't just tasks; they're ways of saying, "You have a future. You are more than what happened to you."

And something beautiful happens. She begins to smile. She begins to play. She may still have nightmares. She may still flinch when touched. But the light comes back, bit by bit.

The safe house becomes a place of transformation, not because it erases what happened but because it proves that healing is possible, that love, consistent and patient, can rebuild a life.

Not every story ends neatly. Some girls return to their families. Some remain under protection for years. But all of them, in their own way, begin again.

STANDARD PRACTICES ACROSS INTERNATIONAL SAFE HOUSES AND RESTORATION CENTERS

The moment a girl is rescued from trafficking, the healing process begins—but it's not quick, and it's not simple. Recovery isn't a straight line. It's a careful, intentional process that unfolds over time, often in stages:

1. **Immediate Safety and Stabilization**

   The first and most urgent need is safety. Rescued children are taken to a secure, confidential location where they're protected from further harm. Basic needs—food, shelter, clean clothing, hygiene, and medical care—are met immediately. Often, girls arrive malnourished, exhausted, and traumatized.

2. **Establishing Trust and Predictable Routines**

   In the early days, the focus is on calm, consistency, and care. Survivors aren't pressured to talk about their experiences. Instead, they're introduced to daily routines—mealtimes, school, chores—that help restore a sense of normalcy. Predictable rhythms help the nervous system begin to relax.

3. **Trauma-Informed Care**

   Professional caregivers trained in trauma recovery offer emotional support in gentle, noninvasive ways. This includes access to trauma-informed therapy, but it often begins with play, art, or story-based methods. The goal is to rebuild a sense of safety within the body and the mind.

4. **Medical and Psychological Assessment**

   Each girl receives a comprehensive medical evaluation, including testing for infections or injuries resulting from abuse. Mental health support is tailored to the individual, addressing anxiety, depression, PTSD, dissociation, and other trauma responses. Medication may be used if appropriate.

5. Education and Empowerment

Most children arrive years behind in school. On-site education helps them begin to catch up at their own pace. Life skills are also taught, like hygiene, nutrition, boundaries, and emotional regulation. These lessons are framed not just as academics but as tools for reclaiming agency and confidence.

6. Peer Relationships and Community

Healing doesn't happen in isolation. Being part of a community of girls who understand one another creates a powerful environment for recovery. Play, conversation, shared meals, and support groups foster healthy relationships and the re-learning of trust.

7. Reconnection or Reintegration (if appropriate)

In some cases, efforts are made to reunify the child with safe family members, but only after thorough evaluation. If not possible, long-term foster care, group care, or even adoption may be considered. Reintegration is slow and supported, always prioritizing the child's safety and well-being.

8. Long-Term Aftercare and Advocacy

Healing is a lifelong journey. Even after leaving the rescue center, girls are offered continued support through therapy, education sponsorships, vocational training, and mentorship. The goal is not just recovery, but restoration. The hope is that each child will not only survive but thrive.

CHAPTER 9
CHALLENGES AND REFLECTIONS

> "Some volunteers cry and feel like they failed.
> But your heart breaking for us? That's a gift."
> Survivor of sex trafficking

EMOTIONAL TOLL AND BURNOUT

As much joy and hope as we witnessed, there were also days that left us with heavy hearts. Volunteering at a rescue center isn't always a smooth experience, filled with smiles and victories. There are moments. And it's those moments when we were grateful we did this as a team.

An experience like this brings your "emotional toolbox" to the table. Each of us has been challenged by the emotional weight placed upon us at one time or another. Sadness, anger, despair, and grief surfaced. We felt guilty for not doing more, but were also too drained to move another muscle at times. Yes, these are all experiences that can become quite real and are magnified when you're away from the safety net provided by your home, family, and friends.

"Oh, goodness, look at that sweet girl," I whispered to my teammate sitting next to me on the edge of the stage, watching the kids come through the door.

"Oh Lord, she couldn't be more than five years old!" She lowered her head and clasped her hands together, her eyes welling up with tears. "It looks like she has been groomed to be sold today."

This very young girl stood near the back of the room, her blank stare revealing nothing. Bright pink lipstick and rosy cheeks, bright blue eye shadow—none of it looked normal. The makeup was more of a neon sign screaming at all of us in the room: *Please help me!*

We sat frozen for a moment, our hearts aching and unsure of what to do with the storm of emotions rising in our chests. Everything in us wanted to scoop her up, wipe away the makeup, and carry her to safety, but that wasn't our role.

We weren't there to investigate, intervene, or fix what we didn't fully understand. That responsibility rested with the trained staff and counselors, who knew how to act with wisdom and authority and had earned the community's trust.

Our role, in that moment and every moment, was to love each of those kids, to create a space that felt safe, even if just for an hour, to offer laughter, play, and the simple kindness of being seen without judgment.

And so, we smiled gently when she looked our way. We made space beside us on the floor, encouraging her to sit by us. We waited to see if she'd join the game. We trusted that even a few minutes of joy could plant a seed. We prayed she'd be protected, and we knew the watchful eyes of the staff would see what we saw—and more.

I still think about that little girl. I don't know what happened next. It left us horrified—and for me, it left a hole in my heart. I couldn't fix it. I wanted to. I'm sure we all did. Everything in me screamed: *Do something!* But instead, I had to let go and trust. That's one of the most complex parts of this kind of service—holding the tension between heartbreak and hope, between action and surrender.

Sometimes, showing up with love is the most powerful thing we can do. And sometimes, it's the only thing we're meant to do.

FINDING HOPE AND LETTING GO OF DESPAIR

Even on the hardest days, when burnout threatened to take over, there were small practices and moments of clarity that helped us keep moving forward.

There were days when despair whispered louder than hope. But somehow, every time, something pulled us back. Despite the heaviness, hope was always present— sometimes in tiny moments.

By working as a team, although it would've been easier at times to sink into that rabbit hole, we chose to hold on to hope. We kept circling back to our task at hand: pour love on those kids; give them a reason to hope.

Hope is a choice, not a feeling. And it's worth choosing.

SAFETY AND MEDICAL EMERGENCIES

Volunteering in a third-world country comes with risks. It's normal for any volunteer to wonder, when contemplating a trip like this: *Will I be safe? What if I get sick?*

Earlier, I wrote about preparation. The team made sure to discuss these issues *before* we left home.

SAFETY

We had one rule which we lived by on each trip: NEVER go anywhere alone. No exceptions. All excursions, restaurant meals, shopping, and other activities were undertaken as a team or in small groups. Early to bed. Common sense dictated.

MEDICAL EMERGENCIES

Again, *preparation is key.* You'll be required to buy travel insurance and, in some instances, "evacuation insurance" in the event of a medical emergency.

You'll have seen your primary doctor and received any required vaccinations, depending on your travel destination. Being prepared includes a complete physical examination. Your doctor will confirm that you're well enough to make the trip. Do not overlook this step!

Pack a supply of all the remedies you normally rely on routinely (i.e., cold medicine, stomach medicine, pain relievers, etc.). If you're warned not to drink the water, honor that recommendation to the letter. Sometimes, that even means don't put your face in the shower!

Finally, and very importantly, team leaders require a complete health form before departure, which includes all essential medical information, a list of all the medications you're taking, and personal contact information in case of a medical emergency. Again, do not overlook this step!

BEST LAID PLANS

Even with the best preparations, things don't always go as planned. On our last trip, about a day before we were to return home, I fell ill.

There's something about having a health emergency in a foreign country, and especially in a third-world country, where healthcare may be in question. It's very frightening, which adds to the stress for both the "patient" and the team. Planning is essential.

It was an *exceptionally* hot day, and we played extra hard with the kids that day, knowing that our time with them was coming to an end. Every day was exceptionally hot. I became severely dehydrated, and my blood pressure rose to a dangerous level.

I was chatting with my teammate, Cindy, in the room where we stored all the puppet supplies, about the wonderful day we had with the kids. Suddenly, my legs gave out from under me, and I dropped to my knees. I felt very faint.

"Cindy, please get Diane for me," I recall mumbling through nervous tears.

Diane oversaw our health histories and was prepared to act if needed. I remember feeling so grateful that Diane knew me so well and knew my health history. That is not always the case, and that's why solid preparations are so necessary.

You'll find that most rescue centers like this one have medical staff on site. This is something you want to determine before you go, so you have a plan in place if there's no medical help nearby. In our case, there was a certified nurse on site.

Diane and Cindy took me to the nurse's office. He smiled, staring into my eyes as if he were trying to read my condition, and asked me a few questions, none of which I remember. He took my blood pressure more than once. Finally, he unlocked an old medicine cabinet bolted on one of the walls and scanned the labels of all the medications (written in his language) with his index finger, settling on one which he explained was a type of blood pressure pill. He wrote down its specifics on a small piece of paper and gave me two extra tablets for the next couple of days.

This is where trust plays a significant role. My anxiety was obvious.

"Susan, I must remind you that I have helped dozens of volunteers from the United States and other parts of the world. You are not the first volunteer to succumb to the heat and humidity," he laughed. I knew he was right.

He was a certified nurse in his country and felt confident that I'd be fine. I trusted his judgement.

I returned to the hotel early that evening, and by the next day, I recovered enough to travel.

I saw my primary doctor shortly after my return to the States. She agreed that, fortunately, the nurse gave me the proper medication for the situation.

"Given what I know now, and considering where you traveled, I must say I would have prescribed a different blood pressure medication for you. Next time, make sure and tell me exactly where you're going!" my doctor advised.

I suppose the takeaway here is that you never know what might happen. I want to emphasize the importance of good planning and preparation when going to a third-world country. Take all the precautions seriously. Have a thorough discussion with your doctor beforehand to confirm that your medications, which may be suitable in your climate at home, will be effective in a different environment.

PRACTICAL SKILLS THAT HELPED

We didn't always have the perfect coping strategies, but over time, a few simple practices helped us hold steady in the middle of it all.

Debriefing with teammates was probably the most essential and powerful tool. Converting the feelings trapped in our hearts into spoken words was often the catalyst that we needed to keep up the good work.

It wasn't about having all the answers. We were all learning each day.

Stepping outside, taking a deep breath, and saying a prayer. It was about simple tools to stay grounded and sane.

MANY PATHS TO SERVICE, EACH ONE EQUALLY VALUABLE

There are many ways to serve. Here are just a few.

Service isn't limited to one place or one kind of work. It ripples out, and the people back home—our families and friends, our communities, our churches—all play an invaluable role in this journey.

When our team started the planning process for our first trip, many people wanted to come with us but couldn't for various reasons. That didn't stop them from playing a key role in the overall success of the first trip and subsequent trips.

PRAYER

I thanked God each day for all those who kept us in prayer, and for those we served, from the moment the mission trip was affirmed to the day we returned home. I believe in the power of prayer. It wasn't uncommon for one or another teammate to express their gratitude for those who prayed for us back home. It mattered, and we felt it.

FUNDRAISING

We established a minimum amount that each team member was responsible for, including their personal air travel and subsistence, and relied on donations for the rest. Without the generous donations of friends, family, business colleagues, and others, we could've never fulfilled the mission. Team members initiated their fundraising efforts, and the team, as a whole, came up with some community events to raise money.

FUNDRAISING EVENTS

PHOTO SHOOT WITH YOUR PET

I'll highlight this one. This was a spectacular success! One of our church members donated her photography services. We held this event at another church member's popular, pet-friendly wine tasting room. Combining friendly pets on leashes and premium wines made for a fun afternoon and a successful fundraiser.

SEWING CAMPAIGN AND CLOTHING DONATIONS

We were blessed by a team of women who coordinated a sewing campaign that created cotton T-shirt dresses for the children. One of the longtime members of the church couldn't come on the trip, but she opened her home to a team of ladies. Some brought additional sewing machines. I still remember that project fondly. It took me back to my love for a TV series, "Little House on the Prairie," loosely based on the book series by Laura

Ingalls Wilder, where all the women circled a large table and made a quilt, all the time gossiping about anyone who hadn't come to the sewing circle! We had a great time, filled with lots of laughter, and created dozens of little dresses to bring along on our mission trips.

CHAPTER 10
DON'T LOOK AWAY
WHEN THE MISSION IS CLOSE TO HOME

CONTENT WARNING:

This chapter contains depictions of grooming, child trafficking, including familial betrayal and exploitation. Reader discretion is advised.

THE TRAFFICKING CRISIS IN THE UNITED STATES

I went halfway around the world to serve children rescued from sex trafficking, and the experience changed me forever. But as I sat down to write this book, I knew I couldn't stop there. The truth is, the problem I witnessed abroad is just as devastating here in the United States. Sometimes, it hides in plain sight.

The children I met were so young—many of them barely able to tie their shoes. I saw firsthand the vulnerability of those at risk or the innocence stolen from others, and learned about the long, brave journey toward healing. And I can't help but wonder: ***How many children right here in our neighborhoods are quietly suffering in the same way?***

We want to believe that this kind of horror doesn't happen "here." But it does. It looks different, yes, but the pain, manipulation, and theft of childhood are the same. And if we care about kids, we can't look away.

This chapter is not about fear. It's about *awareness* and *action*. It's about the courage to learn, listen, and protect. It's about recognizing the subtle ways children are groomed, manipulated, and silenced—and understanding how we, as adults, caregivers, teachers, neighbors, and human beings, can step in before the damage is done.

There is so much we can do. And we must.

Because children everywhere deserve our vigilance, our voice, and our love.

UNDERSTANDING GROOMING: WHAT EVERY PARENT AND GUARDIAN SHOULD KNOW

When we think about child trafficking, we often imagine force or abduction. But the reality—especially here in the United States—is far more subtle and insidious. Most children are not taken by strangers. Instead, they're *groomed* by someone they know.

Grooming is a calculated process predators use to gain a child's trust, lower their defenses, and create emotional dependence. It often happens over weeks, months, or even years. And it's done with one goal in mind: control.

This is what makes grooming so dangerous. At first, it doesn't look like danger. It seems like friendship, attention, and affection—sometimes even love.

Groomers can be:

- Family members
- Family friends
- Teachers or coaches
- Older teens
- Online "friends" who gradually become confidants

They may offer gifts, praise, special privileges, or a listening ear. They may single out a child who is shy, lonely, insecure, or in need of affirmation. Over time, they push boundaries—slowly at first—testing what they can get away with—a hug that lasts too long, a secret shared "just between us," a photo request, a late-night message.

Before a child even realizes what's happening, they're tangled in a web of emotional dependency, secrecy, shame, and confusion. And once abuse begins, many children stay silent—not because they want to, but because they're scared. They don't want to hurt someone they trusted. Or they've been threatened. Or they've been convinced that the abuse is their fault.

GROOMING RED FLAGS PARENTS SHOULD KNOW:

- An adult or older teen spends excessive time alone with your child.

- They give gifts, money, or special privileges without an apparent reason.

- They encourage secrecy ("Don't tell your parents").

- They test physical boundaries—tickling, back rubs, playful "accidental" touches.

- Your child seems unusually attached to or dependent on that person.

- Your child becomes withdrawn, anxious, or unusually secretive.

- They receive texts, messages, or photos that they hide or delete.

WHAT YOU CAN DO:

- **Talk early, talk often.** Teach your child the difference between secrets and surprises, safe and unsafe touches, and real and fake friendships.

- **Keep communication open.** Let your child know they can tell you *anything,* and you will believe them and love them no matter what.

- **Watch behavior more than words.** Trust your instincts—even if the person seems kind, helpful, or well-liked.

- **Model boundaries.** Show your child what healthy relationships look like.

- **Be involved online.** Know who your child is talking to. Monitor social media, gaming chats, and private messages—especially with people they've never met in person.

Grooming thrives in silence. But when we know what to look for—and speak up early—we can stop abuse before it starts. No child should ever be made to feel confused about love, loyalty, or safety.

WHEN TRUST BECOMES A TRAP

Here is a short, fictional story that makes the concept of grooming more real.

Mary was nine years old, shy, kind, and a little lonely. Her parents both worked long hours, and after school, she often stayed with a neighbor, Mr. Jake, who had been part of the community for years. He was friendly, always waved to the other parents, and seemed to genuinely enjoy having kids around.

At first, it was innocent. He gave Mary extra snacks, let her play video games, and told her she was "his favorite." He was the only adult who listened, she thought. Over time, he started to offer her little gifts—hair clips, bracelets, even a new tablet "just for fun." He told her she didn't need to tell her parents, that it could be their "special secret."

Mary felt special. Chosen. Important. But slowly, things changed. Mr. Jake started commenting on how pretty she looked. He wanted more hugs, longer ones. He began showing her pictures she didn't understand. She felt uncomfortable but didn't know how to explain why. He had been so nice—*how could he be doing something wrong?*

She started to avoid eye contact at home and grew quiet in class. One day, a school counselor noticed the change and gently asked Mary about her afternoons. That conversation may have saved her.

WHY THIS MATTERS

Grooming doesn't always look like danger. It often looks like kindness, familiarity, or even friendship. That's why it's so important to teach children that:

- Secrets are not okay when it comes to safety.

- No one—no matter how kind or familiar—has the right to make them feel uncomfortable.

- They can always come to a trusted adult and be believed.

LENA'S SECRET ONLINE FRIEND

Here's another fictional story that describes online grooming.

Lena was twelve, bright, creative, and always drawing. She just started middle school and was still adjusting to the social swirl of adolescence. At home, she spent a lot of time online—mainly drawing, messaging with friends, and playing games.

One day, on a drawing app, a user named "JayDreams" complimented her artwork. He said he was 14 and loved to sketch, too. They started chatting. He was funny and encouraging, always saying the right thing when Lena had a bad day. He told her she was talented, mature, and different from other girls.

Soon, their conversations moved to private messages. He wanted to see more of her drawings, then more of her selfies, even though she wasn't supposed to share pictures online. He told her he liked the way she smiled when no one else was around. He started asking personal questions. He told her he understood her better than anyone else.

He warned her: "If your parents find out about us, they won't understand. They'll take your phone away. They'll think I'm bad, but we know the truth."

Lena didn't know how to respond. She felt nervous. But she also didn't want to lose him—he had become her escape, her comfort.

One evening, her mom noticed Lena flinch when a message notification popped up. She'd grown secretive and irritable, especially when asked about her phone. Something wasn't right.

Her mom didn't yell. Instead, she sat with her and asked, "Is someone online making you uncomfortable?" Lena hesitated, then burst into tears.

That question—and the trust behind it—opened the door.

WHAT PARENTS CAN WATCH FOR IN ONLINE GROOMING

Groomers use social media, gaming platforms, chat apps, and forums to find and manipulate children. They often build emotional bonds before asking for anything inappropriate.

RED FLAGS IN CHILDREN:

- Suddenly secretive about devices or online activity.
- Switching screens or apps quickly when you enter the room.
- Getting upset if access to devices is limited.
- Receiving gifts, games, or money from unknown sources.
- Withdrawal from family or friends, mood swings, or anxiety.

RED FLAGS IN ONLINE INTERACTIONS:

- Messages from older users with compliments or personal questions.

- Requests for photos or private chats.

- Conversations that include secrecy ("Don't tell your parents").

- Emotional manipulation ("I thought you cared about me").

- Quick shifts from friendship to affection or control.

WHAT YOU CAN DO AS A PARENT OR GUARDIAN

- **Talk early.** Teach your child about safe vs. unsafe online behavior, just like you teach them about crossing the street.

- **Keep communication open.** Make sure your child knows they can talk to you without fear of punishment.

- **Monitor, don't spy.** Use parental controls but also build trust. Ask, "Who are you chatting with these days?"

- **Model healthy boundaries.** Discuss consent, privacy, and what real friendship looks like—even online.

- **Be curious, not accusatory.** If something feels off, approach them with care: "You've seemed a little off lately. Is everything okay?"

Online grooming can happen to any child in *any* household. The best defense is a strong connection with your child, paired with the courage to talk about hard things.

HOW YOU CAN HELP: PROTECTING CHILDREN IN YOUR COMMUNITY

You don't have to be a parent or a professional to protect children. Sometimes, the most powerful thing you can offer is your *presence*—your eyes, your voice, your willingness to pay attention.

Many children who are groomed or trafficked fall through the cracks, not because no one cared, but because no one watched closely enough. We can change that.

HERE'S HOW YOU CAN HELP:

- **Learn the signs.** You've just read about grooming. Share that knowledge with others—especially teachers, neighbors, youth leaders, and coaches.

- **Look out for the kids around you.** If a child seems unusually quiet, anxious, withdrawn, or overly affectionate with an older teen or adult, pay attention. If something feels off, it probably is.

- **Speak up.** If you see a red flag, don't dismiss it. Report suspicious behavior. Ask gentle questions. Your voice might be the only protection that a child has.

- **Create safe spaces.** Whether you're a neighbor, faith leader, mentor, or a coach, be the adult a child knows they can trust. A single healthy relationship can interrupt a grooming pattern.

- **Encourage community programs.** Support schools, nonprofits, and after-school initiatives that promote awareness, boundary-setting, and digital safety for kids.

Trafficking doesn't start with kidnapping. It often begins with loneliness, vulnerability, and misplaced trust. When we build strong, caring communities where children feel seen, valued, and safe, we push the traffickers out.

You don't have to do everything. But you *can* do something. And sometimes that something is precisely what a child needs.

RESOURCES FOR FAMILIES, EDUCATORS, AND ADVOCATES

It can feel overwhelming to know where to begin, but you don't have to figure it out alone. Many outstanding organizations are doing life-saving work to prevent child trafficking, educate communities, and support survivors.

The Resources section at the end of the book offers a list of trusted, U.S.-based organizations offering resources for parents, guardians, educators, and anyone who wants to be part of the solution. Whether you're looking for prevention training, survivor stories, or a place to report a concern, these groups are here to help.

A FINAL WORD

You don't need to be an expert—you just need to care.

Learn the signs. Start the conversation. Share what you know.

Because when even one child is protected, it's worth everything.

CHAPTER 11
MY PROMISE TO YOU

> "Don't forget us, even after you go home.
> Please don't forget."
> Survivor of sex trafficking

I close my eyes and inhale as deeply as I can. Exhaling slowly, I open my eyes and look out the window at the trees dancing to a summer breeze. I smile and take another breath.

It feels so good to have written this book. Finally, so much time has passed since our last trip in 2019, but the tug on my heart never wavered. I made a promise to myself that even if I could never go back, I'd do whatever I could to help in the fight against child abuse and sex trafficking. This book is one way.

Fingers resting on the keyboard, I stare out the window, thinking,

Have I left anything out?

Can you feel what I felt when I first looked into the eyes of those little ones?

Do you understand their vulnerability?

Do you see that this is happening all over the world?

Do you understand how love can heal and transform lives?

Do you see that, yes, you can help, and in doing so, your life will change forever?

I rest my head in my hands for a moment, checking in with my heart.

We brought them new faces to brighten their days, fresh songs to lift their spirits, and new games to spark joy. More importantly, we offered them an unbroken chain of love, hope, and safety. When our time came to leave, I think the only way I could say that last goodbye was to imagine that new team taking their seat on the edge of the stage.

They stare at each other, wide-eyed, hearing those feet scramble up the stairs as dozens of little souls race to be first in and first to jump into the laps of unsuspecting newbies. First, to stare into the eyes of faces so different from theirs. First to feel what over-the-top joy feels like, knowing that they are safe. First, knowing it's okay to be first, because there is enough love here to go to the moon and back!

I will never forget!

We will not be silenced!

To anyone reading this and wondering if they're enough—if they have what it takes to volunteer in a place like this—I want to say, from the bottom of my heart, you do. You are enough. You don't have to be perfect. You don't have to be fearless. Just show up—with compassion, humility, and love. The kids will show you the way. And that, I promise you, is more powerful than you can imagine.

And if traveling to a rescue center in a third-world country isn't something you can do, please know this: you don't have to go far to find ways to help. Trafficking and exploitation are happening in neighborhoods and communities all over the world, including right here at home. Vulnerable children and families exist in every zip code. Shelters, advocacy groups, food banks, foster care programs, and prevention initiatives all need compassionate hearts and helping hands. Whether across the ocean or across the street, your presence matters.

I mentioned that I compiled 29 questions to ask before you embark on a mission trip. I have one more:

What good works are being prepared in you, that a greater purpose might be fulfilled through you?

My prayer for each of the dear ones I had the honor to meet:

May your generation grow up stronger than the one before.
May you always know that you are deeply loved.
You matter.
Follow your dreams.
You can do anything you set your mind to.
You deserve the very best that life has to offer.
And know this—no matter how far away we are, you will never be forgotten.
I carry your light in my heart, always.

With love,

Susan

RESOURCES

RESOURCES FOR SUPPORT AND ASSISTANCE

If you or someone you know is experiencing or has experienced abuse, trafficking, or exploitation, help is available. The following organizations offer support, information, and crisis response services:

1. **Childhelp National Child Abuse Hotline (U.S.)**

   Website: www.childhelp.org/hotline

   Phone (available 24/7): 1-800-4-A-CHILD (1-800-422-4453)

   Offers confidential crisis intervention, information, and referrals to thousands of social service, emergency, and support resources in the U.S. and Canada.

2. **Global Human Trafficking Hotline – Polaris Project**

   Website: www.humantraffickinghotline.org

   Phone (U.S.-based, but resource-rich globally): 1-888-373-7888

   SMS: Text "HELP" or "INFO" to 233733

   Supports victims of trafficking and connects individuals with local services. Polaris also provides links to global anti-trafficking organizations.

3. **ECPAT International**

Website: www.ecpat.org

An international network of organizations working to end the sexual exploitation of children around the world. Their site provides country-specific resources and contacts.

WHERE TO LEARN MORE AND GET HELP

National Center for Missing & Exploited Children (NCMEC)
Website: https://www.missingkids.org
1-800-THE-LOST (1-800-843-5678)
Help for families of missing or exploited children, with prevention tools and safety guides.

National Human Trafficking Hotline
Website: https://www.humantraffickinghotline.org 1-888-373-7888
Text "BEFREE" (233733)
Confidential, 24/7 support for victims, families, and concerned citizens. Offers multilingual help.

Darkness to Light
Website: https://www.d2l.org
Training for adults on preventing, recognizing, and responding to child sexual abuse.

Thorn
Website: https://www.thorn.org
Tech-based solutions to stop online child sexual abuse. Includes digital safety resources for families.

Love146
Website: https://www.love146.org
Focuses on prevention education and long-term survivor support—excellent resources for schools.

Shared Hope International
Website: https://www.sharedhope.org
Advocates for stronger laws, offers training, and provides reports on child sex trafficking in the U.S.

Polaris Project
Website: https://www.polarisproject.org
Runs the trafficking hotline and offers extensive research, survivor-centered policies, and data tools.

CyberTipline (via NCMEC)
Website: https://report.cybertip.org
Report suspected child exploitation, online grooming, or explicit content involving minors.

MISSION TRIP VOLUNTEER CHECKLIST

LOGISTICS AND PREPARATION

- What are the travel arrangements, and who is responsible for booking them?

- Do I need a passport, visa, or other documentation?

- What vaccinations or health precautions are required or recommended?

- What should I pack (clothing, toiletries, supplies, gifts, etc.)?

- What is the cost of the trip, and what does it include (lodging, food, transportation)?

- Are there fundraising options or financial assistance available?

- Will we have access to a phone or the internet during the trip?

PROJECT AND PURPOSE

- What is the primary mission or focus of the trip?

- What kind of work will we be doing daily?

- Who are we serving, and how were their needs identified?

- How does this trip support ongoing or long-term efforts?
- Are we working in partnership with local organizations or leaders?

SAFETY AND HEALTH

- What are the safety and security conditions of the area?
- Is there access to medical care in case of illness or injury?
- Will we be covered by travel/health insurance or need to arrange our own?
- How are clean drinking water and food handled?

CULTURAL AND ETHICAL CONSIDERATIONS

- What cultural norms, customs, or dress codes should I be aware of?
- Are there local language basics I should learn?
- How should I approach taking photos and sharing stories of people we meet?
- What is the local view of foreign mission groups or volunteers?

TEAM AND LEADERSHIP

- Who is leading the trip, and what experience do they have?
- Will there be training or orientation before we go?
- Who do I talk to if I have questions or problems during the trip?
- Will we be having group devotionals, reflections, or team-building activities?

SPIRITUAL AND PERSONAL PREPARATION

- How can I prepare spiritually for the trip?

- What emotional or mental challenges might I face?

- Will there be time for journaling, prayer, or reflection during the trip?

- Will there be a debriefing session after the trip?

- How can I stay involved or support the mission after we return?

READING LIST

*Ministering Cross-Culturally, An Incarnational Model for
Personal Relationships,*
by Sherwood G. Lingenfelter and Marvin K. Mayers

Stop the Silence: Thriving after Child Sexual Abuse,
by Dr. Pamela J. Pine

*Voices Against Trafficking: Courage is Contagious: Uniting Voices
and Nations in the War Against Human Slavery,*
by Andi Buerger, JD

A Path Appears: Transforming Lives, Creating Opportunity,
by Nicholas D. Kristof and Sheryl Wu Dunn

*Half the Sky, Turning Oppression into Opportunity for Women
Worldwide,*
by Nicholas D. Kristof and Sheryl Wu Dunn

Don't Look Away: Saying Yes to the One,
by Don Brewster

ACKNOWLEDGEMENTS

> ### Myth #4: We can go it alone.
> Brené Brown, *Daring Greatly*

My deepest gratitude goes to Dr. Pamela J. Pine, author of *Stop the Silence* and a tireless advocate in the fight against child sexual abuse and trafficking. I'm honored that you agreed to write the foreword to this book. Your decades of work in prevention, education, and policy have shaped global conversation, and your willingness to lend your voice to this project is a gift beyond measure. Through your insights and expertise, you offered a broader context I couldn't have fully grasped from my perspective as a volunteer at a rescue center. Your contributions helped strengthen this book and highlight my call to action.

To Diane Blalock—a trusted friend whose presence has spanned the years, thank you for standing by me on this journey. Your support of my writing, your willingness to dig into memories with me, and your thoughtful perspective on our shared experiences made this book stronger and truer. You are, in every sense, a friend I can count on—and I'm blessed beyond words for that.

To my teammates: Diane, Karen, John, Allison, Jordan, Margie, Meg, Cindy, Debra, and Eliza—your willingness to share your reflections and takeaways in this book added depth and soul that only lived experience can offer. To you and all the members of our team, we were more than a team—we were a family in motion, looking out for each other while pouring love into the lives of children who needed it most. I will never forget the joy, the tears, the late-night talks, and the laughter we shared. What we did together mattered. These are the memories of a lifetime, and I carry them with deep gratitude and love.

To Jennifer Sproul—though our friendship is just a couple of years old, your presence in my life has felt like the gift of an old soul. In that short time, you've become a wise mentor and a steady encourager. Your belief in me helped free my spirit and gave me the confidence to write this book. I'm deeply grateful for your insight, laughter, and unwavering support.

To Laura Di Franco and the entire team at Brave Healer Productions—thank you for your professionalism, your fierce dedication to helping authors speak brave words, and your unwavering belief in the power of healing through story. Your expert guidance turned my vision into reality, and your team walked me through every step with grace and encouragement. Laura, as both publisher and daughter, you've worn both hats with strength, humor, and heart—and I'm in awe of the work you've built and the lives you've touched.

To my daughters, Laura and Alissa—you have both been a wellspring of inspiration, love, and support. Laura, thank you for your invaluable writing coaching and your encouragement, if not downright pushing me down the path to completion! Alissa, your deep wisdom, calm spirit, and fierce heart continue to teach me how to listen and love with more presence. You've both cheered me on, held space when I doubted myself, and reminded me of my purpose when I needed it most. I am endlessly proud to be your mom.

ABOUT THE AUTHOR

Susan Ernst is a mother, grandmother, and lifelong advocate for the well-being of children. Her recent journey into writing was born from a life spent caring deeply—from operating a small daycare while raising her two daughters, to volunteering at a rescue center for trafficked children halfway around the world. Her heart for service and healing runs deep.

For five years, Susan traveled each year with a dedicated team of volunteers to serve children rescued from—or at risk of—sex trafficking. These mission trips inspired her to write *Called to Serve: Standing with Survivors and Protecting Children Still at Risk,* her first solo book, as both a testimony and a call to action for others who feel drawn to serve, and to raise awareness about the global crime of sex trafficking and child abuse.

Susan's career as a real estate consultant and appraiser has spanned 37 years. She founded her real estate appraisal practice in 1990 and plans to retire at the end of this year with gratitude for a spectacular career, to embrace full-time authorship, and to explore what life in this new season has to offer. She is an accomplished technical proofreader for Brave Healer Productions and offers her proofreading services to authors around the world.

Susan is a contributing author to all three volumes of *Brave Kids: Short Stories to Inspire Our Future World-Changers,* where her stories focus on empowering children with tools to face fear and build resilience. She is also a collaborating author in the recently released *Gifts of Wisdom: Practices for Healing and Empowerment*. Susan recently attended a writers' retreat in Ireland, where a new book collaboration was born: *The Alchemy of Intuition: Embodied Practices to Access Your Inner Voice*, led by Dr. Tiffany McBride. Susan's chapter, "Find Your Soul-Self: Healing the People Pleaser Problem," will be released in January 2026 on Amazon.

Now living on the East Coast, Susan finds joy and inspiration in long walks in nature, family gatherings, connecting with dear friends in California, and the camaraderie found within the Brave Healer author community. One of her greatest pleasures is watching her two grandchildren—now young adults—as they begin to explore life on their terms and find their way in the world.

She is the proud mother of two daughters, both of whom have dedicated their lives to helping others.

CONNECT WITH SUSAN:

Website: https://www.susanernstauthor.com
Facebook: https://www.facebook.com/sernst992/
Email: sernst992@gmail.com

CALL TO ACTION

"We must protect the child, for the child is the hope of the future. If we destroy the child, we destroy the future of the family, of the nation, of the world."

Mother Teresa

You have walked with me through these pages, and I hope you have felt the tug on your heart. The truth is, children in every corner of our world need us—our time, compassion, voices, and love.

Not everyone can travel across the globe, but each of us can do something. Perhaps it is volunteering close to home, giving financially to organizations that serve tirelessly day and night, or sharing what you have learned so others may join in the work.

I ask you to pause here and consider: *What can I do?* Can I give a few hours of my time? Can I offer resources? Can I raise awareness in my community?

We cannot all do everything, but each of us can do something. And when we do, children's lives are changed forever.

I invite you to step forward. When we reach out to the most vulnerable, we discover a deeper truth: in lifting them up, we lift up ourselves.

If you are ready to explore next steps, I invite you to visit www.susanernstauthor.com. There you will find a list of rescue facilities around the globe, as well as resources and opportunities to serve, give, and spread awareness. Together, our love can become action.

www.ingramcontent.com/pod-product-compliance
Lightning Source LLC
Chambersburg PA
CBHW061806120626
46550CB00005B/2167